CROWDING

IN

REAL

ENVIRONMENTS

D1175476

Edited by

Susan Saegert

(S) SAGE PUBLICATIONS   *Beverly Hills / London*   1976

The material in this publication originally appeared as a special issue of ENVI-RONMENT AND BEHAVIOR (Volume 7, Number 2, June 1975). The Publisher would like to acknowledge the assistance of the special issue editor, Susan Saegert, in making this edition possible.

For information address:

SAGE PUBLICATIONS, INC.
275 South Beverly Drive
Beverly Hills, California 90212

SAGE PUBLICATIONS LTD
St George's House / 44 Hatton Garden
London EC1N 8ER

Printed in the United States of America

International Standard Book Number 0-8039-0583-1

Library of Congress Catalog Card No. 75-42756

FIRST PRINTING

CONTENTS

INTRODUCTION

The papers in this issue all deal with the effects of various levels of density or crowding on people using or living in real environments. The approaches represented are unusual in a number of ways: first, none of the investigations reported employed either of the two most common methods of studying such questions: (1) correlations of aggregate public statistical density measures and measures of pathology, or (2) laboratory experimentation. Instead, people living in dormitories, prisons, ships, and hospitals, and experiencing department stores and railroad terminals were observed, questioned, measured for blood pressure levels, and tested on various cognitive and social tasks. By dismissing public statistics and purely correlational techniques, the authors avoided inaccuracy and lack of refinement in the measurement of variables as well as the problems of suggesting causal links in a purely correlational analysis. The employment of real settings allowed these investigators to sidestep the problem of the external validity of their work; further, the true complexity of the impact of density comes through much more clearly as a result of investigations of it in real-life contexts. Both the papers by Wolfe and by Dean, Pugh, and Gunderson indicate the multiple meanings and effects associated with varying levels of physical density and psychological crowding. To my knowledge, the Wolfe paper is the only longitudinal observational study of the effects of residential density available thus far.

Second, all the authors in this collection demonstrate an acute awareness of the many important distinctions that need to be made in the definition of both density and crowding. While all the authors treat crowding as a psychological variable, Rapoport presents the argument that density itself has a number of psychological components such as perceived density and affective density. In his theoretical paper addressed directly to issues of planning and design, he suggests that the effects of density may reflect not only variations in the number of occupants and space available, but also perceptions of potential density, symbols and associations of density, and sociocultural definitions of density. The papers by Baum et al., Dean et al., Saegert et al., and Wolfe each present evidence corroborating the utility of these distinctions.

The explanatory model of the effects of density most related to the various papers concerns information overload. Saegert, Mackintosh, and West have attempted to discover whether overload does in fact occur in high density situations, and under what circumstances such overload leads to stress. Baum and his colleagues and D'Atri use the model in interpreting the results of their studies of high density living environments. Baum and his colleagues particularly emphasize the design solutions indicated by such a model for ameliorating the negative effects of high density. One of the most interesting possibilities raised by this set of papers is that different types of responses are related more or less directly to physical density, whereas others are almost entirely determined by norms, attitudes, and expectations. For example, the two studies involving physiological measures by D'Atri and by Dean et al. reveal a stronger association between physical density and high blood pressure and illness than between density and subjective measures such as perceived crowding and social affect.

The main conclusion suggested by this collection of articles is that research on density has indeed progressed greatly in the past several years. Density and crowding are now viewed as systemic variables having meaning only in the context of ongoing activities, norms, goals, and physical settings. Rather than leading to confusion, the increased complexity of these approaches seems to be producing a more refined and more explanatory understanding of how different numbers of people and amounts of space shape the course of events and emotions in various, different situations. Certainly this greater sensitivity to context should provide designers and planners with more useful guidelines dealing with density than the simpler, but often inaccurate, formulations of the recent past.

—SS

TOWARD A REDEFINITION OF DENSITY

AMOS RAPOPORT *is Professor of Architecture and Anthropology at the University of Wisconsin at Milwaukee and currently a Research Professor there. He has written extensively on man-environment interaction with special emphasis on synthesis, theory, and cultural variables.*

The concept of density is of central importance in planning, urban design and architecture. There is an extensive literature on it and much discussion of the merits or demerits of specific densities and comparisons of them. It is my suggestion that at the moment density is not a very useful concept in human terms because it is seen largely as a matter of *number of people per unit area* and this is not a very useful approach. It seems necessary to develop some new conceptual approaches to the problem which would enable a redefinition of the term and hence would increase its usefulness. In this essay I will reexamine the concept of density and suggest some possible guidelines for a redefinition.

DENSITY AND CROWDING

There recently has been some extensive reexamination and redefinition of the concept of crowding (Stokols, 1972, 1973; Stokols et al., 1973; Esser, 1971a, 1971b, 1972; Desor, 1972; Kutner, 1973). Yet while crowding is clearly related to density, that latter concept has not received similar attention. At the same time, the distinction between density and crowding continues to be recognized, and there have been two principal ways of distinguishing between them:

(a) Density can be seen as a site measure, and crowding as a measure of density within the dwelling.

(b) Density can be seen as a measure of people per unit area, and crowding as a negative perception of excessive density—a subjective experience of sensory and social overload.

Many of the new definitions of crowding are related to the second of these—to notions of overload, excessive interaction, and the like. These redefinitions, then, hinge on the concept of the *negative subjective experience* of certain density levels. In most work the stress has been on the experience of excessively high density levels. The negative subjective experience may also be of excessively low degrees of interaction, i.e., of too low densities which we may call isolation for want of a better term. It thus seems that crowding defined as a subjective experience is somehow related to density. Presumably, the latter is a more objective measure of the presence of other people and their distribution in space.

Yet it is precisely the degree of this objectivity which I question. I will argue that density itself is a perceived experience and should be seen as more than the number of people per unit area, bedrooms per unit area, and similar ratios. Even in the case of animal populations this simple quantitative statement of population density is not enough to forecast effects and feelings of crowding. Other factors involved are how individuals respond to other members under specific conditions, previous experience, and social organization. For example, clear, stable hierarchies which reduce tension and maintain order and stability also reduce the effects of numbers and thus change the effective density (Dubos, 1965: 105; Leyhausen, 1971). At the regional scale, in the case of human populations, it seems clear that the number of people per unit area is not a good predictor of effective density (Dubos, 1965: 283).

Thus, a concept of density based on a simple ratio model does not seem adequate to predict either behavioral or subjective consequences, and the experience of density must go beyond such ratios. At the very least, density comprises two components—we shall see later that there are many more—and these are the number of people present in an area and the space available per person (Saegert, 1973) which may be related to their interpersonal distance (Kutner, 1973), although I would argue that it is functional rather than physical distance which determines the effective density (Festinger et al., 1950; Whyte, 1956). At the heart of both density and crowding seems to be an awareness of other people through all the senses and, directly or through physical cues, a consciousness of the sharing of spaces and facilities, as well as cultural and physical "defenses" which help control this awareness of others.

Therefore, to deal properly with crowding, one needs to reconsider also the meaning of density. If crowding is the subjective experience of excessively high densities, then designers cannot directly affect it or manipulate it. What they can do is to control density in its traditional meaning, and if the relation of this to perceived density is known, and the relationship between perceived density and feelings of crowding or isolation understood, then these latter feelings may become more predictable and might possibly be affected by manipulating perceived density.

DENSITY

The first point to be made is that while density begins with the number of people per unit area, it must go beyond it. At the same time, the definition of these units and the nature of their boundaries are variable and can play important roles. If, at the simplest level, the built environment is a matter of the distances between people and people, people and objects, and objects and objects, as well as the relative permeability of the various separating boundaries, then it is a matter of effective distances and more generally density, as most aspects of urban design, must be examined in terms of relationships among elements (Rapoport, 1969b). It is such relationships—the form of the arrangements of people in space, the defenses they use to control interaction, the nature of the social group, the nature of boundaries, and so on—i.e., the relationships between people and people, people and objects, and objects and objects, which, I suggest, will play a role in the perception of density.

Density can be seen in different ways (Taeuber et al., 1972), but from a man-environment relations perspective it can be seen in two major ways:

(a) Spatially in terms of the perceived environment, where it is the relationship among elements which is important (height, spacing, juxtaposition), so that it may be hypothesized that high perceived density is related to qualities such as a high degree of enclosure, intricacy of spaces, high activity levels, many uses, and so on since all of these tend to result in higher rates of information from the environment itself (Rapoport and Kantor, 1967; Rapoport and Hawkes, 1970; Rapoport, 1971). Given this formulation, areas identical in terms of people per unit area may have very different perceived densities (Rapoport, 1969a, 1969b, and see below).

(b) In terms of social interaction—actual, desired, or perceived. Involved are the various sensory modalities, the mechanisms for controlling interaction levels—spacing, physical elements, territorial boundaries, hierarchy, the size and nature of the group, its homogeneity, rules for behavior, and so on and how the facilities available are used—all of which affect the rates of social interaction.

There are thus two major aspects of perceived density—physical and social—and these are related since they both affect an awareness of other people—either directly or through artefacts. In other words, they are linked through the concept of rates of information.

If, instead of accepting crowding as the psychological effect of some objective measure of density, I argue that both are subjective and perceived, are not these two concepts confounded again? Wherein is the difference between them?

The difference is the following. Density is the perception and estimate of the number of people present in a given area, the space available, and its organization, whereas crowding or isolation (which we could call affective density) is the evaluation or judgment of that perceived density against certain standards, norms, and desired levels of interaction and information. Put differently, affective density is the appraisal of certain

conditions as unfavorable—the perception of the condition itself
is perceived density.

Physical System	Perceived System	Matched	Affective Density
(density in people——►(perceived density) per unit area organized in certain ways)		against norms, desired levels, etc.	isolation ⟵O.K. crowding

Isolation or crowding, then, are specific instances of an
incongruence between perceived density and some ideals.

The context (which is, of course, culturally defined) also
plays a role so that the different expectations about a party or a
waiting room lead to different perceptions of appropriate
density (Desor, 1972), as do the mechanisms controlling the
impact of people on each other and time (long range versus
short range). It has been suggested that in addition to the
number of people in an area, one needs to consider function, so
that what is normal for a gathering may not be for shopping
because the movement of the same people would change the
context (Doxiadis, 1968: 26). This can be generalized even
more. If we add the effects of culture, we may find that in some
cases (e.g., an Eastern bazaar) there is a search for and
acceptance of very high levels of contact and sensory interaction with people and goods which would be quite unacceptable in a U.S. supermarket. This is, of course, an aspect of
crowding, but given the different norms, different levels of
desired interaction (and, indeed, the meaning of "function" and
activity [Rapoport, 1973: 7-8]), they may also affect the
perception of density.

The major question, then, regarding density is how it is
judged. The answer is that, as in the case of any environmental
system, density is "read" (or decoded). Any environment offers
cues whereby people judge its nature, the potential for action
which it offers, and the behavior appropriate to it. It should
follow that certain cues—physical and social—are read and
interpreted as indicating a dense environment, while others tend
to indicate one which is "not dense" irrespective of, or at least
partly independently of, the actual number of people per unit
area.

Here follows a partial list of some of these hypothesized variables, and the suggestion is that not all are needed for environments to be perceived as one or the other. The list of cues, the number needed to judge environments, how they reinforce or cancel each other, and how they relate to traditional measures of density are all topics for research.

Dense	Not Dense
Perceptual	

tight spaces	open spaces
intricate spaces	simple spaces

These terms are, of course, difficult to define at the moment. The can be discussed in terms of complexity (Rapoport and Kantor, 1967; Rapoport and Hawkes, 1970; Rapoport, 1971, 1969a, 1969b). They also seem intuitively clear to most people—admitting that they are a matter of degree and affected by culture, adaptation levels, and so forth.[1]

large building height to space (i.e., a large amount of subtended building in the field of vision)	low height to space ratio (i.e., little subtended building in the field of vision)
many signs	few signs
many lights and high artificial light levels	few lights and low artificial light levels
many people (or their traces) visible	few people (or their traces) visible
mostly man-made (little greenery)	mostly natural (much greenery)
high noise levels	low noise levels
many man-made smells	few man-made smells
many cars—high traffic density and much parking	few cars—low traffic density and little parking

Generally the number of physical, sensory stimuli which indicate the presence of people.

Associational/Symbolic

Tall buildings, apartments or offices may indicate high density even when spaces and other perceptual cues indicate low density.	Low buildings may indicate low densities even if other cues indicate the opposite.
in residential areas the absence of private gardens and entrances	in residential areas the presence of gardens and entrances

The relative impact and importance of perceptual and associational/symbolic cues are important questions.

Dense	**Not Dense**

Temporal Aspects

fast tempos and rhythms of activity	slow tempos and rhythms of activity
activities extending over the whole 24 hours	activities reducing or ceasing at certain times

Physical/Sociocultural

the absence of "defenses" allowing the control of interaction (Rapoport,1973a)	the presence of "defenses" allowing the control of interaction

Generally, then, the same number of people in an environmental configuration which exposes them to others, or isolates them, would be read very differently (e.g., the presence of fences, court-yards, compounds, and the like).

high levels of "attractive stimuli" (Lipowski, 1971)	low levels of "attractive stimuli"
the absence of other adjacent places for use—streets, meeting places, and so on	the presence of other adjacent places for use—streets, meeting places, and so on

Thus the availability of many nondwelling places—pubs, shops, streets, parks and the like—which can be used by people and whether they are actually used (i.e., the house-settlement system [Rapoport, 1969c]) will affect the perception of density. Where they are present and used extensively, an area would be perceived as less dense because more effective area is available than where only the dwelling area is available for use (Hartman, 1953), and activities are groups may be separated in space and time.

the presence of nonresidential land uses in a residential area and mixed land uses generally	the absence of nonresidential land uses in a residential area and absence of mixed land uses generally

This is in apparent conflict with the previous characteristics. In this case the presence of non-residential uses leads to higher rates of information from the environment itself, more people visible, more traffic, and so forth. There are thus two contradictory effects with complex results.

Sociocultural

high levels of social interaction leading to social overload (Milgram, 1970)	low levels of social interaction and absence of social overload

This depends on culturally (and individually) de-fined desired levels as well as the form and effectiveness of defenses.

Dense	Not Dense
Sociocultural	

Feeling of lack of control, choice, or freedom will lead to judgments of less effective space being available and hence of higher densities. control *by* environment	Feeling of presence of control, choice, and freedom lead to judgments of more effective space being available and hence of lower densities. control *of* environment

The alternative hypothesis, that lack of control means lack of pressure to make decisions and hence the perception of **less** density, is unlikely in view of the evidence that lack of control is associated with increased stress (Glass and Singer, 1972) and with the general argument that density is related to interaction and that privacy is the ability to control unwanted interaction (Rapoport 1973a, forthcoming).

These feelings may differ for various groups—by culture, age, sex, and so on (Skolimowski, 1969; Rapoport, 1968; Raymond et al., 1966; Glass and Singer, 1972; Social Planning Council of Metropolitan Toronto, 1966).

social heterogeneity along some subjectively defined dimensions— hence increased unpredictability, reduced redundancy, and higher effective density in terms of information-processing needs, the inability to read symbols and cues, not sharing rules, and hence acting inappropriately	social homogeneity along some subjectively defined dimensions— hence increased predictability and redundancy and lower effective density in terms of information-processing needs, ability to read cues and symbols, sharing of rules, and hence acting appropriately

One example might be agreement about rules regarding private/public and front/back domains, nonverbal behavior, and so on. This suggests that density and crowding are related via privacy defined as the control of unwanted interaction (Rapoport, 1973a, forthcoming) and also via social norms defining behavior appropriate to various density situations.

absence of culturally shared and accepted nonphysical "defenses" and control mechanisms for regulating social interaction	presence of culturally shared and accepted nonphysical "defenses" and control mechanisms for regulating social interaction
previous experience, socialization, and so forth at low densities (i.e., adaptation level at low densities)	previous experience, socialization, and so forth at high densities (i.e., adaptation level at high densities)

(e.g. Wohlwill and Kohn, 1973)

Thus environments having the same number of people per unit area may be perceived very differently, and on occasion, it may even be suggested that areas with fewer people may be perceived as more dense. I have suggested, using just a few of the variables listed above, that some of LeCorbusier's schemes would be of lower perceived density than some English new towns (Rapoport, 1969b), and some recent French housing projects with large numbers of people per unit area have low perceived density (Rapoport, 1969a). With a more complete set of variables such comparisons would prove extremely useful and would provide a useful way of beginning to relate perceived density to people per unit area.

I have already suggested that both affective density (crowding and isolation) and density may be related through the concept of privacy defined as the control of unwanted interaction, which implies the ability to be alone when one so wishes and with others when that is desired (Ittelson, 1960; Schwartz, 1968; Rapoport, forthcoming). If that is accepted, then many of the cues discussed above can be seen as indicating density through suggesting the presence of actual or potential constraint—either crowding due to an inability to escape interaction (Ledrut, 1968: 100-101, 352) or isolation due to an inability to find people with whom to interact—both evaluated in terms of some desired levels, norms, and so on.

The various categories of cues discussed seem to interact in the process of judging the density of a place. Since there is no work on perceived density, this may need to be approached via crowding. For example, it appears that reduced open space, traffic, industrial and commercial development, and noise are all related to feelings of crowding (Carson, 1972: 165). The presence of "unlike" people has similar effects. Areas possessing these characteristics will then be judged as being of high density while areas having the opposite characteristics will be judged as low density *whatever the number of people per unit area.*

People homogeneous along certain important dimensions (i.e., having similar values, behavior patterns, nonverbal communication systems—in fixed-feature, semi-fixed feature, and nonfixed feature space—the same domain definition, sex and age roles, and so on) have the opposite effect on the perception of density. Because it is easier to disregard others and to take them for granted, an area of given population should be seen as having a lower density when that population is homogeneous than when it is heterogeneous.

In fact, one can see the perception of density and its evaluation (i.e., judgment as isolation or crowding) in terms of expected levels of interaction (as judged from cues) related to both desired levels and actual levels. The ethological literature confirms what is essentially an information-processing view of both density and crowding, as does the literature on privacy and human territoriality. All these streams come together in the literature on boundaries and human territories with their associated rules (Knowles, 1972; Brower, 1965; Lyman and Scott, 1967; Chermayeff and Alexander, 1965: 121-122).

Boundaries can be seen to have three meanings. The first relates to the definition of density in terms of people per unit area. Clearly the choice of areas, i.e., the definition of boundaries, will affect the density in these terms. This has already been discussed and will be elaborated below—it is related to the use of streets, shops, cafes, and like areas for activities which in other cases occur in the dwelling (the house-settlement system) and also to the definition of city limits, census tracts, and so on.

The second meaning relates to physical boundaries—e.g., walls, fences, and curtains. All of these are devices for controlling interaction and information flow and have differing degrees of permeability (varying also with regard to the different sense modalities). In a way they can be seen as filters allowing varying amounts of information to flow in various directions—an informational analogue of the building as climatic filter.

Third, there are social boundaries (Barth, 1970) separating groups, i.e., they tend to separate members from nonmembers, "us" from "them" (which has been suggested as an important function of culture generally). Density will be read differently, and behaviors will be different in their presence or absence. Thus the presence of boundaries appropriate to the context will reduce the impact of one individual on another, will moderate the invasion of, say, personal space, and will allow more people in the same area, i.e., effectively increase density (Baum et al., 1974; Desor, 1972).

Without reviewing the ethology literature, which would be inappropriate here, one can say that each species has its typical spacing (even at low densities) so that it is the distance between conspecifics which is important (Zajonc, 1971) although, as already mentioned, it is the effective distance rather than the physical which is important, and this incorporates the function of barriers and many of the other variables discussed. Among animals, space and social hierarchy are the principal mechanisms for controlling interaction (people, in addition, have physical defenses, cultural rules, and so forth). In all cases, however, the distance between organisms is the result of a compromise between attraction and repulsion, and distance is manipulated by and affects communication (Kummer, 1971; Brereton, 1971). It would appear that fixed and recognized relationships in space, agreed-upon rules (i.e., homogeneity), appropriate cues, symbols and markers, defenses, and so on all have the effect of making behavior more mutually predictable and reduce the need for constant communication in people as in animals. The effect is, then, one of reducing the perceived density since, if we accept the information-processing approach, there are fewer messages per unit time to be processed (whether these messages are social or physical), and these messages are related to the cues discussed above. People and animals both use social hierarchies, familiarity, and eye contact (so that animals are also known to hide behind physical barriers; Kummer, 1971: 226-227). In the case, then, of both people and animals we find behavior substituting for distance.

Thus, as is now well known, it is not "density" which leads to stress if the group is stable, homogeneous, well organized, and able to use appropriate defenses. While under normal conditions there is always some temporary escape, the very different effects of relatives and nonrelatives in Chinese housing are extremely suggestive in this connection (Anderson, 1972; Mitchell, 1971), since the same number of people in this same area have negative effects when they are strangers and do not have such effects when they are defined as kin—i.e., are extremely homogeneous, stable, and well organized. My argument has been that being with like people will lead to lower perceived density. The contrary view is also possible. Being with others, or "them," may lead to isolation because they are depersonalized; one does not interact with "them" and one does not make many fine discriminations about "their" behavior. All this should lead to lower perceived density. However, it seems that since people who are different are seen as threatening and strange, one is always on the lookout for information, for cues, for reassurance. The meaning of behavior and cues given by clothing, gestures, and environmental elements needs to be interpreted and understood (and therefore must be perceived). All of these increase information processing and hence perceived density.

It is a high rate of stimuli which leads to a reading of high density, and their evaluation as unwanted or uncontrollable leads to undesirable effects—i.e., feelings of crowding. Alternatively, it is a low rate of information which is read as low density and, should it be evaluated as too low, may lead to other subjectively undesirable effects. In fact any elements, physical or social, which increase uncertainty, reducing redundancy and demanding attention and increased information processing, lead to increased perceived density. Thus higher numbers of homogeneous individuals per unit area will be read as equivalent to lower numbers of heterogeneous individuals— i.e., as being of lower perceived density.

This argument is also important with regard to boundaries (as a special case of any environmental or social element). In order to be effective boundaries need to be noticed, understood, and finally, obeyed. The first involves the presence of noticeable differences, the second the use of appropriate cues, symbols, and meanings, and the third hinges on the existence of shared rules and norms. In fact, all three work best when there is sharing and agreement. Hence, since effective boundaries reduce perceived density, homogeneity—at least in terms of shared symbols and rules, for example—tends to lead to lower perceived density.

Coming back to the distinction proposed between perceived density and crowding, one finds that density, crowding, and isloation are all related to the need to process information. Density is judged by the amount of information which needs to be processed—total and per unit time—and environmental cues are read as indicators of the rates of likely interactions—they are thus a measure of such interactions and also surrogates for them. Crowding or isolation, on the other hand, is a judgment of the appropriateness of these levels in terms of the presence of unwanted, or absence of wanted, interaction, where the definition of "unwanted," "interaction," and the specific mechanisms used for control are variable and are species specific in animals and culture specific, and more individually variable, in people (Esser, 1971; McBride, 1970; Calhoun, 1966; Desor, 1972; Horowitz, 1965; Pastalan and Carson, 1970; Rapoport, 1973a, forthcoming). As we have already seen, at times withdrawal is sought, and at other times interaction, which will affect judgments of crowding or isolation. Thus, the way in which the elements are organized and related-physically, socially, and temporally—has a major impact on the perception of density and relates a given number of people per unit area to perceived density. This is then judged as acceptable or not, according to certain standards and the availability of various mechanisms for controlling interaction, and leads to feelings of crowding or isolation (affective density; Wynne-Edwards, 1962; McBride, 1964; Pontius, 1967; Wohlwill, 1972; Carson and Driver, 1967; Zlutnick and Altman, 1972; Altman, 1970; Harris and Paluck, 1971; Horvath, 1959).

There is some disagreement about the relative effects of density and/or crowding even in their traditional formulation in terms of which is the more serious, the kinds of effects, whether overload results in overstimulation or withdrawal, and what the effects of excessively low densities (which have been much less studied) might be (Schmitt, 1966; Rosenberg, 1968; Morris, 1967; Mitchell, 1971; Choldin, 1972; LeVine, 1962; Bettelheim, 1971; AMA, 1972; Deutch, 1961; Gottman et al., 1968;

Milgram, 1970; Plant, 1930, 1960; Loo, 1972; Saegert, 1973). It does seem clear, however, as already pointed out, that context plays a role and that space and other facilities available to inhabitants of a very dense area (in the usual sense) will greatly modify both the effect of that density and its perception. Thus, if crowding is cognitive overload and the need very tightly to organize behavior, there may be a difference between the effects of increased group size and the effects due to reduction in the amount of space per person (Saegert, 1973). Similarly, as we have seen, temporal differences, the nature of activities, the constraints of the setting and its symbolism, and the degree of choice all play a role (Harrington, 1965; Proshansky, et al., 1970; Raymond, 1966). These also play a role in the case of very low densities. A group living very widely separated, which has periodic occasions for intense social interaction (say related to festivals, rituals, and the like), would interpret and perceive that density differently, and be affected differently by it than would a group lacking these mechanisms (e.g., compare mining prospectors with Bushmen, Mayans, or tribesmen of the Western Highlands of New Guinea; Rapoport, 1974).

It thus seems clear that there are major effects on the perception of density of social factors such as population homogeneity, kinship, age, sex and sex roles, ritual, activity cycles, extent of home range, and many other types of cultural differences (Mitchell, 1971; Anderson, 1972; Hartman, 1953; Department of the Environment, London, n.d.; Weterle and Hall, 1972). All of these differences and variable effects are due to differences in the use of space and time. For example, stoops, streets, hallways, shops, and other urban elements may be used in one case and not in another (i.e., the availability of the whole neighborhood as behavioral space may vary). There may be a stress on different sense modalities. There may be differences in physical and social control mechanisms available, differences in population characteristics, differences in coming together and moving apart, and differences in the ways in which the environment is structured and organized.

As a result of all these variables, and others, the same number of people per unit area may be perceived as being very different and, depending on how it is judged, very different effects—desirable or undesirable—may follow. This means that the relation of the dwelling to the outside and other elements—the house-settlement system (Rapoport, 1969)—must be considered. While I cannot elaborate this in great detail here, the concept has already been mentioned. It is an analysis of the elements of the environment which are used by people for similar sets of activities. Where and when various activities take place may vary for different groups. The number of settings, their spatial distribution, their temporal relationships, and the rules which prescribe how they are used and by whom lead to very different behavioral spaces and very different relative importance of the dwelling. The result is very different effective and perceived densities.[1]

The nature (permeability) of physical barriers must also be considered as must the nature of rules, i.e., the use of nonphysical elements for the control of interaction (either defenses against interaction or interaction encouraging or facilitating mechanisms), as must the layout and design of the setting. In general, of course, the more people per unit area, the more interaction or potential interaction, but all these factors—dwelling and micro-area design, psychological and cultural mechanisms, social factors—play a role. Areas with identical numbers of people per unit area can have quite different perceived density and be evaluated quite differently to the extent that even in a culture with strong preferences for low density, the more densely settled area may be evaluated as less dense and hence, in this case, more desirable if it is laid out and designed so as to minimize interaction (Wilmott, 1962; Architects Journal, 1973; Yancy, 1971; Bailey, 1970) and if this low interaction is made clear through appropriate cues.

It thus seems clear that it is necessary to go beyond physical space in discussing density to what has been variously called behavioral space, action space, the cognitive space within which a group moves, or whatever (Rapoport, 1970, 1973a). For example, if, within a city, two groups have behavioral spaces A and B, then the same number of people in the similar housing areas will be perceived as being at very different densities in terms of the house-settlement system or behavior setting system. This behavioral space available is also related to the rules about the use of streets as activity space or merely as movement space (Rapoport, 1969c, 1973a). In each case the perception and evaluation of density would be quite different (Hartman, 1953).

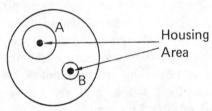

In order to deal with the effects of density, they must be considered in terms of human responses, i.e., as subjective and perceived, principally in terms of the rates of information processing before they are judged against some norms. Assuming that I am correct, and perceived density is different to "objective," then only in this way can meaning be given to terms such as "low," "high," and "medium" density. For example, "high density" in Hong Kong and the United States are represented by very different figures (they are already partly evaluative terms), and it is those that need to be compared. For comparison one must use figures which are true equivalents in terms of their effects, and these may, on the face of it, appear very different. For example, in the United States it has been suggested that 340 square feet per person is a minimum in housing; in Europe the figure is 170 square feet per person, whereas in Hong Kong 43 square feet per person seems to have no undesirable consequences (Mitchell, 1971). At the same time, the social make-up of the group and the form of the dwelling (high-rise versus low-rise) are of great importance in Hong Kong, but in any case one cannot compare a figure of, say, 100 ppa in China, Japan, and the United States as being an identical density—for valid comparison we may have to compare 4,000, 500 and 100 ppa, respectively (although these figures are arbitrary) as being the true equivalents.

The reasons for this follow directly from our discussion. High, medium, and low density seem to be evaluated in terms of certain implicit norms and potential effects. There is an implication that high density means higher rates of information and interaction than low density and hence certain behavioral consequences. But such rates are relative to desired levels and norms, and their effects are based both on these and on perceived density. Also norms and desired levels, as well as perceived density, vary. Considering the cues which play a role in the perception of density, it seems likely that there will be group differences in the perception of density (if only because of the different reading of cues, different sense modalities stressed, and different adaptation levels) and, of course, even greater differences in the norms against which these are judged (Anderson, 1972). These may not be, of course, as large as in the example above.

We have now seen that density seems to be defined in terms of (1) space organization and various physical cues in various sensory modalities, (2) people-interaction, coding, rules, homogeneity, and so on, and (3) the various associational and symbolic meanings of the environment. These are related in several ways—the form of the environment is read in terms of potential interaction, the character of the people involved (Duncan, 1973; Royse, 1969), and more generally, they all lead to information-processing levels which seem to be at the heart of the perception of density and its evaluation as crowding or isolation.

We thus come back to our starting point—there is a difference between density in terms of people per unit physical space, or amount of space per capita, and perceived density. It is perceived density which, judged by some criteria, results in *affective* density (the experience of being crowded or isolated as defined by the individual or group). Finally, it is this latter which leads to the various consequences. The many physical and social variables which we have discussed seem to play a major role in the perception of density thus linking measures of people per unit area to perceived density and finally to affective density.

Let us consider merely one example—density in the context of Chinese culture. We soon find that many of the variables discussed play a role. In Chinese culture there are strict rules about behavior in various spaces and interaction. Norms stress the desirability of large numbers of people sharing dwellings; privacy is defined in terms of groups not individuals; family and nonfamily are treated very differently (Anderson, 1972). The same space in the dwelling with the same number of people is perceived very differently and evaluated very differently in terms of its affective density depending on whether the people are kin or nonkin (Anderson, 1972; Mitchell, 1971). The form of the dwelling and its relation to the street also play a role so that high-rise buildings, particularly their upper stories, are evaluated very differently with upper stories seen as undesirable and have different behavioral effects than do low-rise, or lower stories, mainly through the control of children (Mitchell, 1971; Schak, 1972). This is related not only to the use of streets, shops, and the outdoors generally to get away which is difficult on upper stories (an example of the house-settlement system), but also the the control of children not only by parents, but also by the larger group. This requires certain spatial configurations allowing group members to see children under specific sets of conditions—a situation also found in the case of certain groups in the United States (Hall, 1971). I have not fully developed this example here, and there are many other striking examples from other cultures, but the complexity and multi-dimensional nature of density and the need for a high level of specificity are very striking. Insights into this matter can also be obtained if one considers what happens if certain changes occur in either the social or physical environment even though the number of people per unit area remains the same. For example, destroying social networks and ethnic enclaves increases stress and individual autonomy. This results in higher perceived density due to the presence of "others" and "strangers" and a greater need for attention and information processing on the part of the individual, which leads to increased affective density and possibly stress. Any change which increases the awareness to a potential interaction, the need to process social or environmental interaction at levels greater than the desired or accustomed levels, leads to higher perceived density and, if evaluated negatively, to higher affective density (crowding). The reverse is true if information-processing levels are reduced.

The various social mechanisms employed at levels of high affective density (crowding) have received attention from social scientists. The physical devices which can play a similar role have received far less attention. If we define privacy as a method of controlling unwanted interaction, then we can list a number of possible devices—physical distance (spacing), physical defenses (walls, doors, locks, curtains, and the like), social rules (hierarchy, manners, avoidance behavior, and so forth, all of which predetermine who interacts with whom, makes interaction more predictable, and thus reduces unwanted interaction), separation in time (this can be through scheduling, separate roles, and so on), internal (psychological) withdrawal, and so on (Rapoport, 1973a, 1974, forthcoming). All of these, as well as the specific elaborations of them (some of which have already been discussed) play a role in the perception of density, and an even larger one in the control of interaction and hence affective density.

For example, in Japan we find a clear separation of public and private domains both physically (a turning inward) and socially—very different rules apply in the public and private realms. We find the city broken up into many small areas where people are well known (i.e., are not strangers). There is a clear hierarchical and predictable set of rules for behavior. The house-settlement system contains many stress-reducing elements—such as entertainment areas, inns, baths, and so forth. There are also psychological withdrawal devices (e.g., drunkenness) and physical withdrawal in the house and garden, and within the dwelling, an increase in the effective space available through time scheduling and many other devices (Rapoport, 1969c; Canter and Canter, 1971; Smith, 1970; Meyerson, 1963). We thus see that physical elements are important and also that the various systems work together in terms of both perceived and affective density. It is, of course, clear that these are not the only mechanisms which affect perceived density—in the Netherlands a very different cultural code is used (Bailey, 1970). One extreme example is the use of large and uncurtained windows—the purpose of which is, apparently, to stress that there is nothing to hide, and one need, therefore, not wonder what goes on. Internal psychological withdrawal is also used a great deal as a defense mechanism.

In all these cases the perception of density is thus related to an awareness of cues indicating other people, and many social and environmental factors affect the perception of interaction. They also play a role in judgments about unwanted or insufficient interaction and hence information-processing levels—excessive or inadequate (and their effects).

CONCLUSION

The main thrust of this rather condensed argument has been that although density has not been adequately investigated, it is clearly more than the number of people per unit of physical space, although this must be the starting point. There have been several themes:

(a) the great complexity of the concept of density;

(b) the central role of perception in transmitting sensory data to people and hence in their evaluation of density in terms of information processing;

(c) the existence of cultural and other differences in the desire for, and tolerance of, interaction and involvement, in the definition of "unwanted interaction," and in the ability to control and cope with various levels of interaction, hence the differential judgment of affective density (crowding or isolation);

(d) the presence and use of a large number of physical and social mechanisms which modify density in terms of people per unit area and provide the basis for the cues whereby density is perceived and judged.

It is suggested that density is best seen in terms of its perception and in terms of information processing and that crowding is a specific case of excessively high affective density (excessively high social or sensory stimulation rather than lack of space). Similarly isolation is a condition of inadequate social and sensory stimulation. These two extremes of affective density, then, are similar to the extremes of overload and deprivation more generally. The likelihood that these can only be interpreted in terms of cultural contexts makes extremely hazardous the use of Hong Kong data to judge the likelihood of behavioral sink phenomena in the United States. Nor is it useful to argue, as has been done, that U.S. density figures can go up drastically because they are so much higher in Japan. It is essential to consider in detail, and to a high degree of specificity, the relationship of given sociocultural groups to traditional density figures (people per unit area), the relationship of the particular area to the larger context, the specific activities taking place and their meaning, the detailed layout and design of the setting in terms of privacy (as defined here), the facilities available, the social characteristics of the area in terms of life style, homogeneity, the social rules available and used, and so on before density can be defined and the next step of evaluating it is tackled.

Given the emphasis in the literature on crowding, we can say that crowding is excessively high affective density, i.e., undesirably high perceived density, when the various mechanisms for controlling unwanted interaction with other people are no longer working and all the cues indicate potential interaction demanding attention. Those design features, rules, laws, and so forth which reduce interpersonal perception (direct or by medium of environmental information), also lower the perception of density—hence lowering affective density (i.e., reduce feelings of crowding).

Returning to the two major components of perceived density (information from the environment directly and in terms of human interaction), it can be argued that in a dense area the effects of social interaction (actual or potential) are compounded by sensory inputs and cues from the physical environment—lights, sounds, noises, smells, movement—which demand attention in themselves and which are also surrogates for, and indicators of, human presence—and hence potential interaction. (This view is strengthened by the fact that in wilderness areas the extraordinary richness of sensory stimuli does not seem to be ever read as density—this only happens with man-made environments.)

Nothing in this argument changes any of the findings on crowding. It merely introduces an intermediate step in the argument allowing for cultural and personal differences. In dealing with the negative effects of density, one finds that the variable is perceived density, and this is basically the way people "read" the cues indicating the number of people per unit area. There will need to be a clear understanding of the relation of these various physical cues and the effects of social and cultural factors such as homogeneity and life style on the perception of density and on its evaluation—leading to affective density and its effects. Unchanged, although needing much more understanding, is the range of mechanisms which modify the effects of density on people and the defenses which are available and can be used by specific groups (Zehner, 1970; Cassel, 1972).

It seems clear that while much of the literature stresses the negative effects of high densities, there are also undesirable effects of low densities—both are effects of specific levels of affective density. A useful analogy may be with sensory overload at one end and sensory deprivation on the other. Somewhere in between, for any given group and context, there is a limited range of acceptable and preferred densities as perceived. Any definition of density must allow for this factor.

NOTE

1. These, and a number of other aspects of this topic, will be developed in more detail in a forthcoming book by Rapoport on man-environment aspects of urban design.

REFERENCES

ALTMAN, I. (1970) "Territorial behavior in humans: an analysis of the concept," pp. 1-24 in L.A. Pastalan and D. H. Carson (eds.) Spatial Behavior of Older People. Ann Arbor: Univ. of Michigan Press.

American Medical Association (1972) Human Habitat and Health. Washington, D.C. April.

ANDERSON, E. N., Jr. (1972) "Some Chinese methods of dealing with crowding." Urban Anthropology 1, 2 (Fall): 141-150.

Architects Journal (1973) "High density housing." (January): 23-42.

BAILEY, A. (1970) "The little room." New Yorker (August 8): 24, 57 (part 1); (August 15): 32-63 (part 2).

BARTH, F. (1970) Ethnic Groups and Boundaries. London: Allen & Unwin.

BAUM, A. et al. (1974) "Architectural variants of reaction to spatial invasion." Environment and Behavior 6, 1 (March): 91-100.

BETTELHEIM, B. (1971) "Mental health in the slums," pp. 31-48 in The Social Impact of Urban Design. Chicago: University of Chicago Center for Policy Study.

BRERETON, J. L. (1971) "Interanimal control of space," pp. 69-91 in A. H. Esser (ed.) Behavior and Environment. New York: Plenum.

BROWER, S. (1965) "The signs we learn to read." Landscape 15, 1 (Autumn): 9-12.

CALHOUN, J. B. (1966) "The role of space in animal sociology." J. of Social Issues 22, 2 (October): 46-58.

CANTER, D. and S. CANTER (1971) "Close together in Tokyo." Design and Environment 2, 2 (Summer): 60-63.

CARSON, D. H. (1972) "Residential descriptions and urban threats," pp. 154-168 in J. F. Wohlwill and D. H. Carson (eds.) Environment and the Social Sciences: Perspectives and Applications. Washington, D.C.: American Psychological Association.

——— and B. L. DRIVER (1967) "An environmental approach to human stress and well-being; with implications for planning." Ann Arbor: University of Michigan Mental Health Research Institute. (mimeo)

CASSEL, J. (1972) "Health consequences of population density and crowding," pp. 249-262 in R. Gutman (ed.) People and Buildings. New York: Basic Books.

CHERMAYEFF, S. and C. ALEXANDER (1965) Community and Privacy. Garden City, N.Y.: Anchor.

CHOLDIN, H. M. (1972) "Bibliography: 'Population Density', 'Crowding', and 'Social Relations'." Urbana: Univ. of Illinois Department of Sociology. (mimeo)

Department of the Environment (n.d.) London. Ongoing study on the evaluation of six housing estates.

DESOR, J. (1972) "Towards a psychological theory of crowding." J. of Personality and Social Psychology 21: 79-83.

DEUTCH, K. (1961) "On social communication in the metropolis." Daedalus 90, 1 (Winter): 99-110.

DOXIADIS, C. A. (1968) Ekistics. London: Hutchinson.

DUBOS, R. (1965) Man Adapting. New Haven: Yale Univ. Press.

DUNCAN, J. S., Jr. (1973) "Landscape taste as a symbol of group identity." Geog. Rev. (July): 334-355.

ESSER, A. H. (1972) "A Biosocial Perspective on Crowding," pp. 15-28 in J. F. Wohlwill and D. H. Carson (eds.) Environment and the Social Sciences: Perspectives and Applications. Washington, D.C.: American Psychological Association.

——— (1971a) "Towards a definition of crowding." Sciences. New York: New York Academy of Science (October).

——— [ed.] (1971b) Behavior and Environment. New York: Plenum.

FESTINGER, L. et al. (1950) Social Pressures in Informal Groups. Stanford, Calif.: Stanford Univ. Press.

GLASS, D. C. and J. E. SINGER (1972) Urban Stress. New York: Academic.

GOTTMAN, J. et al. (1968) "Images of the future city." Ekistics 25, 150 (May): 288-289.

HALL, E. T. (1971) "Environmental communication," pp. 247-256 in A. H. Esser (ed.) Behavior and Environment. New York: Plenum.

HARRINGTON, M. (1965) "Resettlement and self image." Human Relations 18, 2 (May): 115-127.

HARRIS, E. G. and R. J. PALUCK (1971) "The effects of crowding in an educational setting." Man-Environment Systems (May).

HARTMAN, C. W. (1953) "Social values and housing orientation." J. of Soc. Issues 19, 2 (April): 113-131.

HOROWITZ, M. J. (1965) "Human spatial behavior." Amer. J. of Psychotherapy 19: 20-28.

HORVATH, F. E. (1959) "Psychological stress: a review of definitions and experimental research." Yearbook, Society for General Systems Research (Vol. 4).

ITTELSON, W. H. (1960) Some Factors Influencing the Design and Function of Psychiatric Facilities. Brooklyn, N.Y.: Brooklyn College Department of Psychology.

KNOWLES, E. S. (1972) "Boundaries around social space: dyadic responses to an invader." Environment and Behavior 4 (December): 437-445.

KUMMER, H. (1971) "Spacing mechanisms in social behavior," in J. F. Eisenberg and W. S. Dillon (eds.) Man and Beast: Comparative Social Behavior. Washington, D.C.: Smithsonian.

KUTNER, D. H., Jr. (1973) "Overcrowding: human responses to density and visual exposure." Human Relations 26, 1: 31-50.

LEDRUT, R. (1968) L'Espace Social de la Ville. Paris: Editions Anthropos.

LeVINE, R. A. (1962) "Witchcraft and co-wife proximity in SW Kenya." Ethnology 1: 39-45.

LEYHAUSEN, P. (1971) "Dominance and territoriality as complemented in Mammalian social structure," pp. 22-33 in A. H. Esser (ed.) Behavior and Environment. New York: Plenum.

LIPOWSKI, Z. J. (1971) "Surfeit of attractive information inputs: a hallmark of our environment." Behavioral Science 16, 5.

LOO, C. M. (1972) "Effects of spatial density on social behavior of children." Man-Environment Systems (November).

LYMAN, S. M. and M. B. SCOTT (1967) "Territoriality, a neglected social dimension." Social Problems 15: 236-249.

McBRIDE, G. (1970) "Social adaptation to crowding in animals and men," pp. 142-166 in S. V. Boyden (ed.) The Impact of Civilization on the Biology of Man. Canberra: Australian National Univ. Press.

——— (1964) A General Theory of Social Organization and Behavior. Vol. 1. (University of Queensland, Faculty of Veterinary Science.) St. Lucia, Australia: Univ. of Queensland Press.

MEYERSON, M. (1963) "National character and urban form" Public Policy 12: 78-96.

MILGRAM, S. (1970) "The experience of living in cities." Science 167 (March 13): 1461-1468.

MITCHELL, R. E. (1971) "Some social implications of high density housing." Amer. Soc. Rev. 36 (February): 18-29.

MORRIS, D. The Human Zoo. London: Jonathan Cape.

PASTALAN, L. A. and D. H. CARSON [eds.] (1970) Spatial Behavior of Older People. Ann Arbor: Univ. of Michigan Press.

PLANT, J. S. (1930) "Some psychiatric aspects of crowded living." Amer. J. of Psychiatry 9, 5 (March): 849-860.

PLANT, J. S. (1960) "Family living space and personality development," in N. W. Bell and E. F. Vogel (eds.) A Modern Introduction to the Family. Glencoe, Ill.: Free Press.

PONTIUS, A. A. (1967) "Neuro-psychiatric hypotheses about territorial behavior." Perceptual and Motor Skills 24 (June): 1232-1234.

PROSHANSKY, H. M. et al. (1970) "Freedom of choice and behavior in a physical setting," pp. 173-182 in H. M. Proshansky et al. (eds.) Environmental Psychology. New York: Holt, Rinehart & Winston.

RAPOPORT, A. (forthcoming) "Socio-cultural aspects of man-environment studies," in A. Rapoport (ed.) The Mutual Interaction of People and their Built Environment: A Cross-Cultural Perspective. The Hague: Mouton.

——— (1974) "Nomadism as a man-environment system." Presented at a conference on Psycho-Social Consequences of Sedentarization, UCLA. December. (mimeo)

(1973a) "Some perspectives on human use and organization of space." AA Q. 5, 3 (July-Sept): 27-37.

——— (1973b) "Images, symbols and popular design." Int. J. of Symbology 4, 3 (November): 1-12.

——— (1971) "Designing for complexity." AA Q. 3, 1 (Winter): 29-33.

——— (1970) "The study of spatial quality." J. of Aesthetic Education 4, 4 (October): 81-95.

——— (1969a) "Housing and housing density in France." Town Planning Rev. 39 (January): 341-354.

——— (1969b) "The notion of urban relationships." Area (J. of Institute of British Geographers) 3: 17-26.

——— (1969c) House Form and Culture. Englewood Cliffs, N.J.: Prentice-Hall.

——— (1968) "The personal element in housing: an argument for open-ended design." RIBA J. (July): 300-307.

——— and R. HAWKES (1970) "The perception of urban complexity." AIP J. 36, 2 (March): 106-111.

RAPOPORT, A. and R. E. KANTOR (1967) "Complexity and ambiguity in environmental design." AIP J. 33, 4 (July): 210-221.

RAYMOND, H. et al. (1966) L'habitat Pavillonnaire. Paris: Centre de Recherche d'Urbanisme.

ROSENBERG, G. "High population densities in relation to social behavior." Ekistics 25, 151 (June): 425-427.

ROYSE, D. C. (1969) "Social inferences via environmental cues." Ph.D. dissertation. MIT. (unpublished)

SAEGERT, S. "Crowding: cognitive overload and behavioral constraint," pp. 252-260 in W.F.E. Preiser (ed.) Environmental Design Research: EDRA 4. Vol. 2. Stroudsburg, Pa.: Dowden, Hutchinson & Ross.

SCHAK, D. C. (1972) "Determinants of children's play patterns in a Chinese city: the interplay of space and values." Urban Anthropology 1, 2 (Fall): 195-204.

SCHMITT, R. C. (1966) "Density, health and social disorganization." AIP J. 32, 1 (January): 38-40.

SCHWARTZ, B. (1968) "The social psychology of privacy." Amer. J. of Sociology 73, 6 (May): 741-752.

SKOLIMOWSKI, H. K. (1969) "Human space in the technological age." AA Q. 1, 3 (July): 80-83.

SMITH, R. A. (1970) "Crowding: the Japanese solution." Landscape 19, 1: 3-10.

Social Planning Council of Metropolitan Toronto (1966) A Preliminary Study of the Social Implications of High Density Living Conditions. April 4. (mimeo)

STOKOLS, D. (1973) "The relation between micro and macro-crowding phenomena: some implications for environmental research and design." Man-Environment Systems (May): 1-11.

——— (1972) "A social-psychological model of human crowding phenomena." AIP J. 38, 2 (March): 72-83.

——— et al. (1973) "Physical, social and personal determinants of the perception of crowding." Environment and Behavior 5, 1 (March): 87-115.

TAEUBER, C. et al. (1972) Density: Five Perspectives. Washington, D.C.: Urban Land Institute.

WETERLE, G. and E. R. HALL (1972) "High rise living: can the same design serve young and old." Ekistics 33, 196 (March): 186-191.

WHYTE, W. H. (1956) The Organization Man. New York: Simon & Schuster.

WILMOTT, P. (1962) "Housing density and town design in a new town." Town Planning Rev. (July): 115-117.

WOHLWILL, J. F. (1972) "Behavioral response and adaptation to environmental stimulation," in A. Damon (ed.) Physiological Anthropology. Cambridge, Mass.: Harvard Univ. Press.

——— and I. KOHN (1973) "The environment as experienced by the migrant: an adaptation level view." Representative Research in Social Psychology 4, 1 (January): 135-164.

WYNNE-EDWARDS, V. C. (1962) Animal Dispersion in Relation to Social Behaviour. Edinburgh: Oliver & Boyd.

YANCEY, W. L. (1971) "Architecture, interaction and social control: the case of a large-scale public housing project." Environment and Behavior 3, 1: 3-21.

ZAJONC, R. B. (1971) "Attraction, affiliation and attachment," pp. 143-166 in J. F. Eisenberg and W. S. Dillon (eds.) Man and Beast: Comparative Social Behavior. Washington, D.C.: Smithsonian.

ZEHNER, R. B. (1970) "Satisfaction with Neighborhoods: The Effects of Social Compatibility, Residential Density and Site Planning." Ph.D. dissertation. University of Michigan. (unpublished)

ZLUTNICK, S. and I. ALTMAN (1972) "Crowding and human behavior," pp. 44-60 in J. F. Wohlwill and D. H. Carson (eds.) Environment and the Social Sciences: Perspectives and Applications. Washington, D.C.: Amer. Psych. Assn.

TWO STUDIES OF CROWDING IN URBAN PUBLIC SPACES

SUSAN SAEGERT *is an Assistant Professor at the Graduate Center of the City University of New York, in the Environmental Psychology Program. Her research has included field and laboratory studies of crowding, a study of the redesign of a psychiatric ward in a large urban hospital, and work on the differential experiences of girls and boys in the development of environmental competence.*

ELIZABETH MACKINTOSH *is a member of the Environmental Psychology Program of the City University of New York Graduate Center. Having received a Master's degree in city planning from New York University, she has been employed by the New York City Housing Development Administration. Her main research interests concern problems of housing.*

SHEREE WEST, *also a member of the Environmental Psychology Program at the City University of New York Graduate Center, is interested in the areas of recreational planning, leisure environments, children's media presentations of the environment, and information processing in environments.*

In the past few years, an increasing amount of research has been directed toward discovering the psychological effects of high density. Most people who have lived in cities and have used crowded facilities find high density situations at least somewhat annoying some of the time. The question remains whether the effects of high densities are more significant than the transient frustration of waiting in lines, standing on subways, or finding that the movie one wanted to attend is sold out. The urgency for evidence on density effects is increasing. With rising construction and land costs in urban centers, developers call for revisions in zoning regulations to permit the construction of more units per site than presently allowed. The ill-housed need sound replacement housing. Conservationists advocate preservation of open space in outlying fringe areas. Present inhabitants of urban neighborhoods claim that increased densities will put an unbearable strain on already overtaxed neighborhood services. Caught in these conflicts, planners and policy makers must nevertheless make numerous decisions. Perhaps now the social sciences can begin to supply evidence on the effects of various densities so that these can be more rational decisions.

The evidence that high density animal populations develop social and physiological pathologies is quite strong (Chitty, 1952; Christian, 1970; Christian et al., 1960; Davis, 1971; Green and Larson, 1938; Green and Evans, 1940; Keeley, 1962; Morris, 1952; Morrison and Thatcher, 1969; Myers et al., 1971; Southwick, 1967; Susiyama, 1967; Thiessen and Rogers, 1961). Calhoun's work (e.g., 1962) indicates that high density rat populations adequately supplied with resources come to behave in anti-social ways, show signs of physiological disturbance, and display frequent deviant sexual and maternal behavior. These findings have aroused much speculation about the possible effects of density on humans. However, similar effects in humans have not been as regularly associated with high densities. Studies such as those by Loring (1956) and Schmitt (1966) and some of those reviewed by Martin (1967) do suggest an association between high density living and various social and physiological pathologies. In laboratory studies of density, Hutt and Vaizey (1966) and Griffitt and Veitch (1971) found that when room size was kept constant, larger groups of subjects behaved in a more anti-social fashion. Other investigators have not found that high densities had negative social, psychological, or physiological consequences (e.g., de Groot et al., 1970; Draper, 1973; Freedman et al., 1971; Wilner and Baer, 1970). Increasingly, studies are leading various investigators to the conclusion that the level of density in a situation can have psychological and social effects, but that these effects depend on specific characteristics of the space (Desor, 1972), social norms (Stokols et al., 1973), other characteristics of the dwelling unit such as floor height (Mitchell, 1971), or characteristics of the people, for example poverty (Galle et al., 1972) or sex (Freedman et al., 1972). If the social sciences can pinpoint the specific conditions that render high density situations negative, planners and policy makers may be able to accommodate higher numbers of people, if necessary, without creating such negative consequences.

These studies, unlike most field studies, look at the effects of actual experienced face-to-face density rather than measures of density based on area statistics. Even though the spaces studied are experienced only for brief periods, exposure to similar high density situations is frequent and repetitive for most urban dwellers. Effects of these short-term situations would be important to consider in planning such spaces as well as in determining the desired density for housing and offices located where these experiences are common.

In a previous paper (Saegert, 1973), it has been suggested that the two components of density, number of people and amount of space per person, may create different psychological effects, and that these separable effects may interact. When there are more people, the cognitive complexity of the situation is potentially greater because there are more elements and quite often more uncertainty about the behavior of these elements. Such conditions present what Milgram (1970) has termed an overload situation, in which an individual is confronted with more information than can be processed. Therefore, he concludes, some form of adaptation is required. Perhaps a more accurate understanding of the person in a highly populated and heterogeneous environment would be that information processing must follow a different strategy than would be useful in a simpler setting. Less of the total information available in the environment can be processed. If a person engages in an activity that would be aided by a clear understanding of the total social and physical environment, large numbers of copresent others might interfere with the performance of this activity, possibly leading to frustration, poorer performance, or some effort to organize the situation to make it less complex, for example, by forming traffic lanes or creating a division of labor. Milgram lists a number of ways that a person might simplify an overly complex environment through selecting, ignoring, preventing, or failing to respond to information about the social and physical setting.

If information overload does contribute significantly to stress in crowded situations, numerous design and planning solutions might be expected to reduce the negative aspects of crowding. Clear articulation and orientation-facilitating design would be essential for crowded spaces. People should be presented with relatively few choice-points and a clear path for pursuing their goals in the situations. Design and graphic devices allowing the user of a space to develop accurate expectations about what the environment holds would be helpful. Visual and path complexity as well as a surfeit of signs and messages in the environment could be expected to lead to greater stress and less efficient information processing. Buildings and spaces should be grouped so as to keep the number of people the user encounters to a manageable number. The design suggestions Newman puts forth in his book *Defensible Space* all have the function of making an area more knowable; in fact, a greater ability to defend a space may be but one consequence of a clearly organized space.

In contrast, a situation in which the space per person decreases does not necessarily increase the amount of information available in the environment if the number of people remains constant. However, reduced space would probably make that information more salient because it can no longer be as easily ignored or controlled by adjusting one's physical proximity to others. Thus the person's choice of physical movement patterns would be constrained. Further, the amount of stimulation impinging on the person might increase arousal even if an adequate strategy for handling information inputs is achieved. Designers and planners should therefore take care in carefully matching activities to be carried out and space available. Activities or experiences that involve concentration or freedom from irrelevant stimulation such as reading, meditating, or intimate interaction should be shielded from the ebb and flow of the other users of the space. Problems encountered in open schools suggest the need for such design precautions.

This analysis of the separate effects of number of people and space available in a high density situation attempts to specify ways a person's relationship to the physical and social environment is changed because of density conditions. The following studies were performed in two public places representative of generic urban environments that are very densely populated at certain times, a shopping environment and a transportation setting. The studies were designed to determine whether information overload does occur as a result of the high number of people in rather close proximity to each other. If so, does it influence people's emotional reactions or ability to perform on tasks and to accomplish goals? If such exposure is stimulating, greater emotionality might be expected to occur. Increased stimulation would tend to increase arousal. However, the type of emotion, e.g., excitement or hostility, might depend on other characteristics of the setting, the person, and the activity. Schacter and Singer (1962) have concluded that arousal can be labeled in any one of a number of different ways depending on the person's expectations and experiences in the setting. In a highly stimulating environment, the type of emotion may vary, but arousal would tend to increase the intensity of whatever emotions do occur. Therefore, it was hypothesized that subjects would express stronger feelings in the more crowded condition. It was also hypothesized that subjects would have greater difficulty with cognitive tasks both during and after exposure to the high density situation.

STUDY I

This study focused on the problem of attaining cognitive clarity in a crowded situation. The site was a mid-Manhattan department store that had regular periods of high and low density. Subjects were exposed to either a crowded or un-crowded condition. During the experimental period, the subject was forced to focus her attention on the shoes and people that she had to describe. Recall of these would therefore test the subject's focal memory. In contrast, recall of the physical environment and the objects in it would test the subject's memory for incidental facts since she was not required to attend to these items during the experimental period. After the experimental period, subjects were asked to perform several cognitive tasks and to express a number of affective evaluations. We predicted that crowded subjects would have more difficulty controlling their attention and forming a clear picture of the environment than would uncrowded subjects, and we expected subjects in the more crowded conditions to express stronger emotions.

METHOD

Subjects

Twenty-eight female undergraduate and graduate students of New York University and Columbia University served as subjects. Each was told that the research was entitled "Information Processing in a Shopping Setting" and was to understand how people perceive and describe objects and other people in a realistic setting rather than in a laboratory. A subject's period of participation was approximately one hour; each was paid $3.00.

Design

The independent variable in the design is density; the dependent variables are performances on cognitive and affective tasks. The experimenters arranged a time schedule to allow for an equal number of crowded and uncrowded experimental sessions. The uncrowded condition began at 10:00 a.m. on a weekday; the crowded one, at either 5:00 p.m. during the week or 1:00 p.m. on Saturday. Twelve subjects experienced the uncrowded condition, sixteen, the crowded. In the analysis the last three crowded subjects were dropped because, at the end, displays were added making the area physically much more crowded than it had been previously.

Procedure

Each subject was treated individually. On meeting the experimenter at one of the entrances to the department store, the subject was taken to the experimental area, a shoe section on the first floor, and was told that she would be left alone there and was to complete two tasks:

(1) Describe twelve shoes in as much detail as you like. Pretend you are describing them to someone who might buy them. Pick any shoe from anywhere in this shoe section. List the characteristics for each shoe on each of the numbered sheets. Place one or two word descriptions in the spaces provided. Put down as many characteristics as you feel are necessary to describe the shoe adequately. There is no fixed number of characteristics that is either "correct" or "incorrect."

(2) Describe three people in the shoe section in as much detail as you like. Pretend you are describing them so that if someone met them and were to have a conversation with them, he or she would recognize them. Put down as many characteristics as you feel are necessary to describe the person adequately. There is no fixed number of characteristics that is either "correct" or "incorrect."

Try not to spend more than two minutes describing each shoe or person so that by the end of thirty minutes, you will have given descriptions for twelve shoes and three people. There is a clock on the wall to check your time.

As the experimenter left the area, she noted the approximate number of people in the shoe section. After thirty minutes, the experimenter returned to the subject and asked her to point out the location of the shoes and people she had described in the order she had described them. The experimenter noted this information on a map of the shoe section and then took the subject to a relatively secluded part of the store where she administered a series of questions and tasks for about thirty minutes.

The subject was first asked background questions about the size of her family while growing up, the place where she grew up, where she had been living in the last year, and what kind of stores she usually shops in. She was then asked to draw a map of the shoe section (on a blank piece of $8\frac{1}{2}$" x 11" paper) with as much detail as she could remember. She could spend a maximum of five minutes on this task. The subject was then requested to recall as many of the characteristics of the twelve shoes and three people she had described before, in the order she had originally listed them. She was given one minute for each. Finally, she rated her feelings about each shoe and person on a seven-point scale that ranged from "very unlikeable" to "very likeable" and estimated the level of density in the experimental area on a seven-point scale.

RESULTS AND DISCUSSION

The effects of density on incidental memory were striking, while effects on focal recall were slight. Subjects in the high density condition tended to remember somewhat less of their shoe descriptions than those in the low density condition although this tendency was not strong ($t = 1.31$, df = 23, $p <$ .10 [one-tailed]). No differences in recall of people were found. This seems to indicate that some disturbance of memory for the focal task occurs in the crowded condition, but it is not substantial. Length of descriptions of people and shoes were not different in the two conditions. Incidental memory, as measured by the accuracy of maps of the experimental area drawn by subjects, seems to be significantly affected by increased density. The percentage of large objects, such as chairs and display stands, forgotten or misplaced was much higher for crowded subjects than for uncrowded ones ($t = 2.58$, df = 23, p $< .01$ [one-tailed], $p < .02$ [two-tailed]). Also, the subjects in the high density condition used fewer words to label their maps than did subjects in the low density condition ($t = 1.78$, df = 23, $p < .05$ [one-tailed]).

Overall, the high density subjects seemed to have a less detailed and less accurate picture of the area in which they had been working. It appears that they retained less information about the physical environment than low density subjects. There may be several explanations for this. First, although the amount of information about the physical environment remains constant in both situations, the amount of information about people in the crowded condition increases because there are more of them. High density subjects may not be processing information about the physical setting because of the increased availability of information about people. They also may not be able to see all the objects and boundaries of the area necessary for the formation of a clear image of the environment. Second, because performance on the simpler shoe recall task was only mildly affected by crowding, while the more challenging map drawing task was definitely influenced, it may be that people's ability to perform more constructive, creative memory tasks are disturbed by high density while their capacity for more routine recall is not.

The analysis of the total distance subjects walked during the shoe description task showed that, although there was no difference between the amount of distance covered by subjects in the two conditions, the distance covered was much more variable in the high density condition (F = 9.20, df = 10/13, p < .01). This finding may indicate that subjects in the low density condition used approximately the same strategies for performing their task, and the environment probably did not interfere; in the high density situation, subjects' strategies may have varied, or the environment may have structured their alternatives in divergent ways.

Analysis of subjects' ratings of the likeability of shoes and people described was unrevealing. However, a more indirect measure of subjects' affect did show a trend. Each subject's shoe and people descriptions were rated by four judges for the number of positive and negative affective words. (The four judges had an average reliability of .87 with a range from .94 to .82.) Subjects in the high density condition gave somewhat more positive descriptions (t = 1.83, df = 23, p < .05 [one-tailed], p < .10 [two-tailed]). This finding is congruent with other studies indicating that females experience more positive affect in crowded conditions. Freedman and Ehrlich (1971) found that female groups acting as juries gave more lenient sentences in smaller rooms; male juries were more lenient in larger rooms. Similarly, Ross et al. (1972) found that ratings of self and others were more positive in a small room than in a large one for female subjects.

Subjects' subjective estimate of the extent of crowding in the experimental area corresponds highly with the actual number of people who were in the area (r = .763, df = 23, p < .01 [one-tailed]). This indicates that subjects actually experienced the condition of either high or low density as such and that our findings are a result of these conditions and not some other variable.

Because the subjects were extremely similar in background, the relationship between the background questions and crowding were not analyzed.

STUDY II

Because the results from Study I were promising, Study II was initiated to expand the experimental design, the sample, and the types of tasks and tests. As with Study I, Study II exposed subjects to high and low density conditions for thirty minutes during which time they were to perform certain tasks, after which a series of cognitive and affective measures were taken. This experiment took place in the Pennsylvania Railroad Station in mid-Manhattan. To test the differential effects of density, both male and female subjects were used. A device intended to reduce the effects of crowding was introduced: a personal tour of the area by the experimenter who indicated its highlights on a map. It was hypothesized that this orientation would structure and simplify the situation, thereby reducing the complexity of information with which the subject would be confronted. An attempt was made to make the tasks in the railroad station more similar to the kind of activities usually occurring in such an environment.

This study was also intended to explore further the relationship between density-induced overload and affective responses. The direction of affect may often be determined primarily by normative expectations, situational definitions, or previous experiences in the setting. However, it seems likely that when tasks require understanding and manipulation of the environment, the surplus of information and the physical constraints produced by high densities would create frustration and stress. In this study, the tasks subjects were to perform involved finding particular places and information available in the environment as quickly as possible. Both scanning of and movement through the environment were necessary. Therefore, subjects were expected to display more negative reactions in the crowded conditions. To test this hypothesis, other measures of affect were added. And finally, to enable comparisons with other studies on stress (Glass and Singer, 1972), the Stroop Color-Word Test was included. Glass and Singer had found that exposure to noise and shock resulted in a performance decrement on this test.

In summary, we predicted that cognitive and task performance would be poorer in the crowded condition, and that affect would be generally more negative in the crowded condition. Subjects in the oriented condition were expected to be less influenced by crowding. Previous studies (e.g., Freedman et al., 1972) led us to expect a sex by crowding interaction on at least some affect measures.

METHOD

Subjects

Twenty males and twenty females of mixed occupations were selected from volunteers who responded to bulletin board signs, newspaper ads, and sidewalk recruiting. They were told that the purpose of the experiment was to find out how people organize their behavior in places with which they are not familiar. Subjects had to be eighteen to thirty years of age, speak English as their native language, and be unfamiliar with the railroad station site. Unfamiliarity was defined as having been in the station not more than three times, or not within the preceding year. All subjects were city residents. A subject's period of participation was approximately one hour; each was paid $3.00.

Design

Independent variables in the design were density, prior information about the environment, and sex. Natural fluctuations of user density in the setting during a typical day provided the high and low density levels. The low density condition occurred during the time period 10:00-11:30 a.m.; high density conditions existed between 5:00-6:00 p.m. Half of the subjects were randomly selected for each condition. Population counts at different locations were made to ensure that the density level for each subject was not significantly different from the typical range for that time period. The area was too large to count the total population. Amount of information about the environment was manipulated by giving half of the subjects the orientation and map of the environment, while half of the subjects were not so oriented. Dependent variables were cognitive and affective responses and task performance during and immediately after exposure to the information-processing requirements of th experimental tasks.

Procedure

One of the three experimenters worked with one subject at a time. A subject arrived at an appointed time outside the experimental area, was taken to the experimental area by the experimenter, and was given the following introduction and explanation of the tasks:

> This is an environmental psychology experiment. Environmental psychology is the study of people and how they interact with physical and social environments. Psychologists have very little information on how people react to environments and so today, we are asking you to do a series of tasks in this area; afterward we will be asking you about your experience. We will be leaving you here alone for 30 minutes and giving you a list of things to do. Do each task in the order in which it is listed. Work as quickly and efficiently as possible. There are 42 tasks listed. Simply try to complete as many as you can. Do not look ahead at the tasks on the list. It is important that you do them in the sequence in which they are presented. If you find it necessary to ask someone 'for help to complete a task, please circle the number of that task.

At this point, subjects that had been assigned to the oriented condition were given a map and told the following:

> In order to help you get oriented in this area, we are giving you a map; I'll now briefly point out where the things are that are on the map.

The remaining instructions were given to all subjects:

> Don't go beyond Track 13 down there; the newsstand over there and the food place down there.

> Two of the tasks require money. Here is the $.12 which you will need. If you want to check the time, there's a clock. I'll meet you back here at _____.

Subjects were given a list of 42 tasks to perform. The tasks were simple, inconspicuous activities, typical of users' behavior in the area such as locating the ticket counter, finding the sitting area, looking up a phone number, or buying something at a newsstand. The tasks were to be done in order; the sequence was arranged to require a number of traverses within the area. Each task also required minimal written evidence that the subject had indeed performed it.

The experimenter met the subject at an arranged time 30 minutes after the subject began the tasks. If the subject had been oriented, the map was reclaimed. Subjects were asked to describe their feelings or mood during the 30-minute experimental period by rating them on the Nowlis Mood Adjective Checklist (1965). The list of 33 adjectives make up 11 scales: (1) aggression, (2) anxiety, (3) sadness, (4) social affection, (5) skepticism, (6) elation, (7) urgency, (8) concentration, (9) vigor, (10) fatigue, (11) egotism. Subjects were requested to give three words that best described themselves and five words describing the environment. Then they were asked to write a paragraph describing their experience in the environment. Finally, subjects indicated on 7-point scales their evaluation of the environment on 8 dimensions: pleasantness, activity, attractiveness, temperature, comfort, interest, understandability, and orderliness. (Analyses were performed on all measures except the paragraphs. For the latter, the diversity of themes in all conditions did not permit construction of reasonable content-analysis categories.)

Subject and experimenter then left the experimental area and went to a quieter, more secluded place where both could sit during the remainder of the experiment. The Stroop Color-Word Test was given as an indicator of postexperimental effects on cognitive efficiency. This is a 3-part test in which the subject's speed is noted in first, reading a page of color names printed in black; second, naming the color of different colored squares; and third, identifying the color of the printing of an incongruent color name. For example, if the word "blue" is printed in red ink, the subject is to read "red" (Glass and Singer, 1972: 82). Subjects then estimated the density of population in the experimental area. They answered a 28-item true-false test designed to indicate the amount of knowledge retained about objects and relationships in the experimental environment. Even though map drawing may more clearly reflect the subject's total knowledge of the environment, that task could not be used, since a map was employed in some conditions for orienting. Finally, subjects expressed their reactions to the experiment and to the orientation if they were in that condition.

RESULTS AND DISCUSSION

The results of the study indicate that the map orientation had no effect on any of the cognitive, affective, or performance measures. This may show that either the kind of orientation and map used were insufficient, that orienting devices in general make no difference in the kind of environment under consideration and for the kind of measures taken, or that maps simply are not very good orienting devices. This latter possibility is supported by Devlin's (1973) study indicating that children using a map were more confused about a particular space than those experiencing the space naively. Because of the failure of the orienting device, results are presented only in terms of the two other independent variables, density and sex.

Crowding did seem to interfere somewhat with tasks requiring knowledge and manipulation of the environment. Subjects in the high density condition completed an average of 25.05 tasks compared to an average of 28.88 for low density subjects ($F = 2.86$; df = 1/32; $p < .10$).

Recall for details of the physical environment, as tested by the true-false test, did not differ between conditions; both groups correctly answered about 68% of the questions. The true-false test included items relating both to focal and incidental information. Separate analysis of these two types of questions still did not reveal differences between conditions. Subjects answered 75% of the task-related questions correctly and 62% of the incidental memory questions. Study I would lead us to expect no differences between conditions in focal recall, but differences in the incidental recall measure. The true-false test may not be sensitive to differences in incidental memory for two reasons: (1) it is a test of recognition rather than free recall; (2) the items that made up the test may not have touched on differences in information between the two groups.

Our expectations that subjects would experience more negative affect in the high density conditions, given the requirements of the experimental task, were confirmed. Subjects expressed more anxiety in the crowded condition ($F = 9.20$, df = 1/32, $p < .005$). Further, crowded subjects were more skeptical than uncrowded subjects ($F = 14.16$, df = 32, $p < .001$). Although no subjects expressed high levels of sadness, high density subjects stated significantly more of these feelings than low density subjects ($F = 4.75$, df = 1/32, $p < .05$). And finally, crowded subjects tended to describe fewer feelings of social affection than uncrowded ones ($F = 3.37$, df = 1/32, $p = .072$). Males and females seemed to be responding differently to the high density condition on two mood scales; crowded male subjects express more feelings of aggression ($F = 4.03$, df = 1/32, $p = .0503$) and elation ($F = 5.05$, df = 1/32, $p < .05$) than crowded female subjects. The finding for the aggression scale is consistent with the Stokols et al. (1973) finding that males rated themselves as more aggressive in a small room, whereas females rated themselves as more aggressive in a large room (see Table 1). Similarly, Freedman and his colleagues (1972) found that males became more punitive and competitive in crowded conditions, but females did not. In this study, men in general expressed more aggressive feelings than women ($F = 5.09$, df = 1/32, $p < .05$); crowded subjects expressed more aggression than uncrowded ones ($F = 7.20$, df = 1/32, $p < .05$).

Because the adjective checklist has the disadvantage of suggesting words or moods that the subject may not otherwise have thought of and tends to define the subject's feelings in the experimenter's terms, subjects were given the opportunity to describe their feelings in three of their own words. A content analysis was performed on these self-descriptions; each word was put in one of six categories by two judges. Interjudge

TABLE 1
Males and Females Feelings of Aggressiveness in Response to Density

	Low Density	High Density
Males	11.80	9.60
Females	11.92	11.60

NOTE: More aggressiveness is indicated by a lower number.
[F = 4.03; df = 1.32; $p < .0503$]

reliability was .92. The category names and the percentage of all responses falling in each are as follows: (1) feelings of inadequacy (26.77%), (2) concentration (18.58%), (3) positive feelings (15.04%), (4) negative arousal (14.16%), (5) general arousal (11.85%), (6) neutral description (7.41%) and (7) negative physical condition (6.19%). These categories seemed to describe exhaustively the themes appearing in subjects' self-descriptions in the study.

The number of subjects in a condition listing at least one word in a category was compared to the number not giving such a word. Differences between density conditions appeared in the frequency with which subjects used words indicating negative arousal, positive feelings, and feelings of inadequacy. A Fisher's exact test was performed on the "negative arousal" and "positive feelings" scores because there were small frequencies in some cells. Crowded subjects expressed more feelings of negative arousal than uncrowded ones (df = 1, p = .0131). For instance, they described themselves as "tense," "hurried," and "rushed." The "inadequacy" scores permitted a chi-square test. High density subjects more frequently expressed feelings of inadequacy (X^2 = 4.91, $p < .05$). They saw themselves, for example, as "confused," "nervous," and "not too bright." On the other hand, the low density condition elicited more positive feelings such as "relaxed," "pleased," and "important" (df = 1, p = .0098). Evidently, subjects in the uncrowded condition generally felt much better about themselves than those in the crowded situation. An interesting contrast is illustrated by the most frequent self-descriptors given in the two conditions. Crowded subjects most often mentioned the word "rushed" (six times), and "confused" (four), while uncrowded subjects said "busy" (three), and "curious" (three). One drawback of the self-descriptor method is that people may not always freely admit to having socially unacceptable feelings; for instance, this technique did not elicit expressions of aggression, whereas the adjective check list did. The self-descriptions did not reveal any sex differences or sex by crowding interactions.

Differences between subjects in the high and low density conditions in their evaluation of the environment were not as dramatic as the differences in their self-evaluations. Crowded subjects rated the environment as more active on a seven-point scale than uncrowded subjects ($F = 10.63$, $df = 1/32$, $p < .01$). A content analysis of subject-generated environmental descriptions (interjudge reliability equals .85) revealed that high density subjects described their environment more frequently as full of stimulation, for example, "bustling," "fast," and "mobbed" ($t = 2.225$, $df = 38$, $p < .05$ [two-tailed]). A t-test on percentage of responses in this category per subject was permissible here because over half the crowded subjects' environmental descriptors fell into the stimulation category and over a third of the uncrowded ones were in this category. In all, these responses accounted for 45.11% of the total. The most frequently mentioned high density environmental descriptors were "crowded" (ten times), "hectic" (eight), and "noisy" (seven), while the low density ones were "crowded" (seven), "busy" (six), and "noisy" (six). The remaining categories subjects used in describing the environment were characterized as (1) negative descriptions (27.17%), (2) adjectives relating to alienation (9.39%), (3) neutral terms (10.87%), and (4) positive evaluations (7.61%).

As with Study I, subjects' perceptions of the experimental condition corresponded with the experimenter's designation of the level of density. This was illustrated by subjects' estimate of the number of people in the area (F = 6.48; df = 1/32; p < .05) and their reports of crowding (F = 15.50; df = 1/32; p < .001).

The results for the Stroop test, included as a performance measure sensitive to stress, revealed an interesting sex by density interaction trend (F = 3.904; df = 1/32; p < .06). Female subjects in the high density condition performed much worse than females in the low density condition. However, males in the high density condition actually performed better on the test than those in the less dense condition (see Table 2).

If this finding is viewed in the light of the sex-by-density interaction on the aggression scale, the differences might indicate that males adopted a more aggressive, active strategy in this high density situation. Such a strategy may have facilitated rather than interfered with task performance. The correlation between higher aggression scores and better scores on the Stroop test (r = .31; df = 38; p < .05) suggests that some relationship exists, though the correlation is not extremely high. The elation scale is not significantly related to the Stroop scores.

CONCLUSIONS

Together these two studies support the idea that high densities do create psychological effects, at least under certain

TABLE 2
Males and Females Performance on The Stroop Color-Word Test as a Function of Density

	Low Density	High Density
Males	79.30	69.88
Females	67.25	73.56

NOTE: A low score indicates a better performance.
[F = 3.904; df = 1.32; p < .06]

conditions: (1) when the person in the situation must scan the environment and move through it, (2) when high densities are attained by increasing the number of people in a constant space, and (3) when the number of people in the situation is relatively large. While other aspects of the situations investigated may be important also, these three characteristics are most relevant to the hypothesis. Under these conditions, we would expect that psychological effects of high densities would arise from the increased information available in a highly peopled environment combined with the increased salience of that information and the decreased freedom of movement occasioned by physical proximity to so many people.

Support for this hypothesis comes from three findings in these studies. First, the less accurate maps drawn by crowded subjects in Study I suggest that these subjects did not retain as clear an image of the physical environment as their uncrowded counterparts. The fewer words used by crowded subjects to label their maps may also reflect less complete coding of the environment. Second, crowded subjects in Study II tended to perform fewer of the experimental tasks. Since these tasks required both knowledge of where things were located and ability to move through the environment, either greater difficulty in attaining cognitive clarity, constraint of movement, or both could be responsible for the performance difference. Finally, the negative affect displayed by crowded subjects in the second study could be attributed to the frustration and sense of inadequacy occasioned by attempting to attain cognitive clarity in an overly complex and fast-paced environment, when these subjects had to act on incomplete information, and also to move about in an obstructing setting. Subjects in Study II described themselves most frequently as feeling inadequate in the situation and as concentrating very hard. While there were no differences between groups in descriptions of concentration, the crowded subjects felt significantly more inadequate. Further, the major characteristics subjects used to describe the environment involved a sense of movement and stimulation. Although both groups used such terms often in their descriptions, crowded subjects used them more frequently. Overall, crowded subjects seem to have been less able to attain a clear image of the environment and to move about freely when the task required doing so; these disabilities resulted in negative emotional states.

The main qualification of these conclusions arises from the failure of the map orientation in Study II to reduce the effects of crowding and the lack of difference between groups in Study II on the true-false test of knowledge about the environment. While these contradictory findings do cast doubt on the hypotheses, the likelihood that they are due to technical problems is quite high. The use of a map as an orienting device in this situation is, in retrospect, very questionable. Little information directly relevant to the subjects' tasks was given by the map; further, using a map may not decrease the cognitive complexity of navigating through such an environment, as has been found in another study (Devlin, 1973). Because maps were used in the manipulation, the drawing of a map as a test of the subjects' knowledge of the environment was not employed. The true-false test was substituted instead. Because the map drawing allows a subject to use whatever knowledge she or he has, it seems to be a better measure than the true-false test which taps only the subject's knowledge of questions determined by the experimenter.

The effects of crowding on task performance deserve special attention since the use of tasks as measures presents a number of difficulties (Hackman, 1970). For example, the crowded subjects' inability to draw accurate maps may reflect a poststress difficulty in performing complex tasks (Glass and Singer, 1971) and may have nothing to do with their knowledge of the environment. This interpretation of the results of Study I would be compatible with the finding in Study II that crowded female subjects performed more poorly on the Stroop test.

Of course, the data from the Stroop test present further difficulties for interpretation since the males performed better when crowded. Here it seems possible that the males in the study were motivated to try even harder on the test to overcome the effects of stress. The fact that the three experimenters were females similar in age to the subjects may have had something to do with the males' performance on the Stroop. Unlike the experimental tasks, which were done while the experimenter was absent, the experimenter was directly involved with the subject while the Stroop was being administered.

A problem exists in finding tasks that distinguish between overload effects and general stress reaction. Decreased performance on any complex task can be seen as an indicator of heightened arousal rather than specifically related to information overload. This would support the idea, commonly accepted among psychologists (e.g., Fiske and Maddi, 1961; Janis, 1967), that task performance and arousal are related in an inverse U-shaped function. Simple tasks, however, are less influenced by arousal, and the optimal level of arousal is higher. Thus in our studies, crowded subjects' decrements in performance on complex tasks would be attributed to their higher level of arousal; failure of other tasks to indicate differences between crowding conditions would be seen as reflecting the simpler nature of these tasks. Probably the best strategy for future investigations of the overload hypothesis would be to design effective orienting devices; if these reduced the effect of crowding, then the hypothesis would be greatly strengthened.

A task that could be used in the crowded situation itself as a good indicator of either overload or stress would be helpful. Both Study I and Freedman and his colleagues (1971) in their early study used paper-and-pencil tasks; the results of these suggest that when the subject is allowed to focus on a task, performance decrements are unlikely to occur. Perhaps such focusing may even provide a successful way of screening out the environment, thus eliminating potentially stressful experiences.

In past research, the relationship between density and emotional reactions has also been puzzling. On the basis of these two studies and research by other investigators, two generalizations seem warranted. First, the direction of the feelings subjects have in a high density situation will be influenced by norms and expectations for that situation; whatever the type of emotion, it will tend to be stronger in high density settings. Our female subjects in Study I displayed heightened positive feeling in a crowded department store, probably in line with expectations that such situations were enjoyable. Stokols et al. (1973) found that subjects felt less crowded when cooperative rather than competitive norms existed in an experimental situation. The findings of Freedman et al. (1972) that females were more lenient and cooperative whereas males were more punitive and competitive in crowded situations can be interpreted as heightened normative behavior. Females who are expected in our society to be pro-social become more so when crowded; males who are expected to be aggressive and assertive also moved their behavior more in this direction.

Second, the type of activity and task being performed seems to influence affective responses. Some activities require that people scan the environment and organize activities for themselves. Especially if these tasks involve movement, the surplus of information and the physical constraints in the situation will be experienced as frustrating or anxiety provoking. Study II lends support to this idea.

The patterns of results for males in the crowded condition in Study II raise the possibility that styles of task performance may be related to emotional reactions to crowding. Although males and females responded to the high density conditions with similar negative emotions such as sadness, anxiety, decreased social affection, and expression of a sense of inadequacy, males also claimed to be more aggressive and elated. The combinations of aggression and elation in males may be components of males' particular reactions to heightened arousal. However, their better performance on the Stroop test is definitely counter to our expectations. Perhaps reacting to crowding with aggression and/or elation reflects a way of coping with high densities so as to facilitate performance on tasks. The mood scale differences and the relationship of the aggression scale to Stroop scores suggest that males and females were dealing with the situation in somewhat different ways. Because the mood scales were obtained immediately after the experimental task while still in the experimental area, the probability of an experimenter effect is lower. This suggests that the Stroop results may reflect more than male subjects' reactions to the female experimenter. Seligman (1974) found that the few depressed patients who responded to being asked to solve insoluble problems with hostility actually improved their scores on subsequent tasks. This finding was counter to the usual result that enforced helplessness in one situation leads to less effort to deal successfully with subsequent problems (e.g., Seligman, 1974). These findings support the idea that our male subjects' anger at the difficulty of doing the assigned tasks contributed to their better task performance later.

Overall, these two studies indicate that information or decisional overload, as well as physical constraint, limits knowledge of and ability to use the physical environment, that affect increases in crowded conditions, and that when the task requires knowledge of and activity in the environment, negative affect is likely to occur. Future studies investigating the relationship between styles or orientations toward tasks and emotional responses to crowding must be conducted to clarify the specific patterns of reacting to crowding. In high density situations, the affective norms and expectations plus the information and movement requirements of ongoing activities are both important. In addition, the person's strategies for processing information and performing activities, as well as the limitations of an individual's information-processing capacity would also influence task performance and emotions. The interreaction of these different factors deserves further exploration.

The results of these two studies point to some broader implications, both for planners and for social scientists. Our findings indicate that people in high density situations tended to learn less about their environment, to have more negative feelings, especially about themselves, to have greater difficulty moving through and organizing a clear image of their environment, and to be less able to carry out tasks. People in the high density condition described themselves in a negative manner—as inadequate, confused, not too bright, tense, and so forth—even though they were in an experimental (therefore perhaps somewhat less compelling) situation, and only experienced the conditions for thirty minutes. These findings present a picture of less understanding, reduced likelihood of exploration and discovery, and lower self-confidence, all of which indicate greatly reduced freedom of choice and impaired perception of alternatives in an individual's life space. If such strong effects are observed even under these experimental conditions, it would seem to be folly not to consider possible density effects in planning situations which affect people regularly or through a large total portion of their day. It will be critical to consider options available to individuals in the larger urban context surrounding facilities such as housing or means of transportation. Urban residents or workers may experience different kinds of high density situations in the course of a day, and their effects may be cumulative. Not only transportation and shopping settings, but also work environments, recreation, and service facilities may produce their own types of high density situations. Conceivably, these may develop to the point where escape from some form of crowded conditions becomes virtually impossible in an individual's life space.

Planners can begin to consider ways in which increased numbers of people can be accommodated without sacrificing their well-being. Our discussion of crowding suggests that it may help to structure high density situations to reduce or order the amount of stimulation and information confronting an individual, both in discrete situations and over time. Decentralizing services and simplifying large-scale environments might contribute to this. Although introduction of a map in our study did not help, other types of maps, imaginative signs and symbols, or clearly defined spaces may alleviate some negative effects of high density. The goal of such planning and design would not be the stark simplicity of the modern stone monolith; the imperviousness and inflexibility of such structures often makes the task of understanding the environment and carrying out human activities extremely complex. Both information and supports for behavior must be humanly accessible and manageable.

REFERENCES

CALHOUN, J. B. (1962) "Population density and social pathology." Scientific Amer. 206: 139-148.

CHITTY, D. H. (1952) "Mortality among voles at Lake Vyrwy, Montgomershire in 1936-39." Philosophical Transactions of the Royal Society of London B236: 505-552.

CHRISTIAN, J. J. (1970) "Social subordination, population density, and mammalian evolution." Science 168: 84-94.

———, V. FLYGER, and D. E. DAVIS (1960) "Factors in mass mortality of a herd of Sika deer (cerus nippon)." Chesapeake Sci. 1: 79-95.

DAVIS, D. E. (1971) "Physiological effects of continued crowding," pp. 133-147 in A. H. Esser (ed.) Behavior and Environment. New York: Plenum.

De GROOT, I., R. L. CARROLL, and R. M. WHITMAN (1970) "Human health and the spatial environment." Prepared for the Environmental Control Administration of the Department of Health, Education, and Welfare, and the American Public Health Association. (mimeo)

DESOR, J. A. (1972) "Toward a psychological theory of crowding." J. of Personality and Social Psychology 21: 79-83.

DEVLIN, A. S. (1973) "Some factors in enhancing knowledge of a natural area," in W.F.E. Preiser (ed.) Environmental Design Research, Vol. II. Proceedings of EDRA IV conference. Stroudsburg, Pa.: Dowden, Hutchinson & Ross.

DRAPER, P. (1973) "Crowding among hunter-gatherers: The !Kung Bushmen." Science 182: 301-304.

FISKE, D. and S. MADDI (1961) Functions of Varied Experience. Homewood, Ill.: Dorsey.

FREEDMAN, J. L. and P. R. EHRLICH (1971) "Interview by Estie Stoll." Sciences 11: 6 ff.

FREEDMAN, J. L., S. KLEVANSKY, and P. EHRLICH (1971) "The effect of crowding on human task performance." J. of Applied Social Psychology 1: 7-25.

FREEDMAN, J. L., A. S. LEVY, R. W. BUCHANAN, and J. PRICE (1972) "Crowding and human aggressiveness." J. of Experimental Social Psychology 8: 528-548.

GALLE, O. R., W. R. GOVE, and J. M. McPHERSON (1972) "Population density and pathology: what are the relations for man?" Science 176: 23-30.

GLASS, D. C. and J. S. SINGER (1972) Urban Stress. New York: Academic Press.

GREEN, R. G. and C. A. EVANS (1940) "Studies on a population cycle of snowshoe hares on Lake Alexander area." J. of Wildlife Management 4: 220-238.

GREEN, R. G. and C. L. LARSON (1938) "A description of shock disease in the snowshoe hare." Amer. J. of Hygiene 28: 190-212.

GRIFFITT, W. and R. VEITCH (1971) "Hot and crowded: influences of population density and temperature on interpersonal affective behavior." J. of Personality and Social Psychology 17: 92-98.

HUTT, C. and M. J. VAIZEY (1966) "Differential effects of group density on social behavior." Nature 209: 1371-1372.

KEELEY, K. (1962) "Prenatal influence on behavior of offspring of crowded mice." Science 135: 44-45.

LORING, W. C. (1956) "Housing and social problems." Social Problems 3: 160-168.

MARTIN, A. E. (1967) "Environment, housing and health." Urban Studies 4: 1-21.

MILGRAM, S. (1970) "The experience of living in cities." Science 167: 1461-68.

MITCHELL, R. E. (1971) "Some social implications of high density housing." Amer. Soc. Rev. 36: 18-29.

MORRIS, D. (1952) "Homosexuality in the ten-spined stickleback." Behavior 4: 233.

MORRISON, B. J. and K. THATCHER (1969) "Overpopulation effects on social reduction of emotionality in the albino rat." J. of Comp. and Physiological Psychology 69: 658-662.

MYERS, K., L. S. HALE, R. MYKYLOWYCZ, and R. L. HUGHES (1971) "The effects of varying density and space on sociality and health in animals," pp. 148-187 in A. H. Esser (ed.) Behavior and Environment. New York: Plenum.

NEWMAN, O. (1972) Defensible Space. New York: Macmillan.

NOWLIS, V. (1965) "Research with the mood adjective check list," in S. Tomkins and C. Izard (eds.) Affect, Cognition, and Personality. New York: Springer.

ROSS, M., B. LAYTON, B. ERICKSON, and J. SCHOPLER (1972) "Affect, eye contact, and reactions to crowding." University of North Carolina (Chapel Hill) Department of Psychology. (unpublished)

SAEGERT, S. (1973) "Crowding: cognitive overload and behavioral constraint," in W.F.E. Preiser (ed.) Environmental Design Research. Proceedings of EDRA IV conference. Stroudsburg, Pa.: Dowden, Hutchinson & Ross.

SCHACTER, S. and J. E. SINGER (1962) "Cognitive, social and physiological determinants of emotional state." Psych. Rev. 69: 379-399.

SCHMITT, R. C. (1966) "Density, health and social disorganization." J. of the Amer. Institute of Planners 32: 38-40.

SELIGMAN, M. (1974) Personal communication.

SOUTHWICK, C. H. (1967) "Intergroup agonistic behavior." Behavior 28: 182-209.

STOKOLS, D., M. RALL, B. PINNER, and J. SCHOPLER (1973) "Physical, social, and personal determinants of the perception of crowding." Environment and Behavior 5: 87-115.

THIESSEN, D. D. and D. A. RODGERS (1961) "Population density and endocrine function." Psych. Bull. 58: 441-451.

WILNER, D. M. and W. G. BAER (1970) "Sociocultural factors in residential space." Prepared for Environmental Control Administration of the Department of Health, Education, and Welfare and the American Public Health Association. (mimeo)

YERKES, R. M. and J. D. DODSON (1908) "The relation of strength of stimulus to rapidity of habit formation." J. of Comp. Neurology 18: 459-482.

THE ROLE OF GROUP PHENOMENA IN THE EXPERIENCE OF CROWDING

ANDREW BAUM *is an Assistant Professor of Psychology at Trinity College in Hartford, Connecticut. He is interested in the social and psychological aspects of both architectural design and crowding, and is associated with the Human Design Group, a socioenvironmental research and consulting organization.*

R. EDWARD HARPIN *is completing his doctoral studies in the clinical psychology program at the State University of New York at Stony Brook where he is pursuing his interests in environmental design.*

STUART VALINS *is a Professor of Psychology at the State University of New York at Stony Brook. His interests include crowding and psychological effects of architectural design, and he is associated with the Human Design Group.*

Recent distinctions between the physical concept of density and the psychological experience of crowding (e.g., Stokols, 1972; Saegert, 1973) have resulted in a new emphasis in the study of human crowding phenomena. Rather than considering density as a sufficient condition to arouse the perception of crowding, this emphasis suggests that high density leads to perceptions of spatial limitation, social overload, and high interference potential, depending on the particular configuration of personal, environmental, and social elements active in the setting. These intervening elements, which include the physical and social properties of a setting as well as more

AUTHORS' NOTE: *This research was facilitated by a research grant from the National Institute of Child Health and Human Development (HD07545-01). The authors wish to thank Carlene S. Baum for her help in the preparation of this paper.*

personal variables which characterize individuals using the setting, are capable of either intensifying or reducing the impact of high density conditions thereby determining the degree to which crowding is experienced.

Personal attributes, such as an individual's personal space requirements, have been shown to influence the experience of crowding (Dooley, 1974), and other characteristics involving culture and heritage also appear to be active in this process (Hall, 1966). The physical properties of a setting also influence the experience of crowding. Desor (1972) found that by varying the architectural features within model rooms, substantial differences in perceived room capacity and crowding could be obtained. Similar results have been found by manipulating the color and visual content of model rooms (Baum and Davis, forthcoming). Evidence for the influence of social variables on crowding has also been reported; the goals of a group (Cozby, 1973), the structure of a group (Schopler and Walton, 1974), or the general orientation under which a group functions (Desor, 1972) can also influence crowding. Personal, physical, and social variables thus appear to be crucial links between the physical conditions of high density and the experience of crowding.

This paper will focus on the role of group phenomena in the crowding process. Groups are social structures that have the capacity to mitigate harmful or aversive effects of high density, thereby reducing the likelihood that individual group members will experience crowding under such conditions. Group development structures the social environment, and by producing boundaries, group members are shielded from many unwanted interactions from outside the group. As a result, group members are less susceptible to the unwanted and frequently inappropriate social encounters generated in high density settings and are less likely to experience crowding. Group members are also less likely to lose control over their social experiences, as their regulation of these experiences is reinforced by the norms established by the group. Finally, the potential for interference in a setting, which is typically high in dense situations, will be less salient for group members; the structures and channels created by a group to ensure smooth and successful interaction tend to circumvent interference by identifying procedures and patterns of movement which guide the activities of the group. The resulting norms regarding social encounter and the use of space can mitigate adverse effects of high density and can reduce the probability that crowding will be experienced by group members.

CROWDING IN RESIDENTIAL ENVIRONMENTS

A series of studies of residential crowding (Baum and Valins, 1973; Valins and Baum, 1973) have indicated that naturally induced and prolonged exposure to high social density engenders the experience of crowding and causes residents to avoid one another. These studies focused on freshmen as new residents of college dormitories which varied along an important design dimension. The interior architecture of corridor-design dormitories, housing 34 students in 17 double-occupancy rooms arranged along a double-loaded corridor, requires residents to share common areas (lounge and bathroom) with 33 others. The other design, housing residents in 4- or 6-person suites, accommodates comparable numbers of residents in equivalent amounts of space on each floor, but requires residents to share common areas with only 3 or 5 others. This architectural difference was conceptualized in terms of the absolute number of interactions which an individual resident could have in these environments; because of the large number of residents sharing living space in the corridor-design dormitories, the probability that they would encounter others and experience unwanted social encounter was greater than for residents of suite-style housing. Research indicated that residents of the corridor-design dormitories were experiencing crowding and avoiding others on their dormitory floors. In addition, these crowded residents avoided strangers in laboratory settings, experienced greater discomfort in the presence of strangers, and manifested lower thresholds for the perception of crowding. The manner in which space is arranged in these dormitories produces differences in the amount of control each resident can maintain over his social experience, and residents of those buildings in which such control was minimal were socially stressed and avoided social interaction.

DIFFERENTIAL GROUP DEVELOPMENT

Further study has indicated that the development of groups in these environments may be related to the experience of crowding in these dormitories. Residents of the suites are housed in "ready-made" groups of 4 or 6 students, and due to the need to coordinate use of common living space, these groups seem to form close units. Corridor residents, however, are provided with two rather unattractive natural groups; they are housed in a large group of 34 sharing various areas and in groups of two sharing bedroom space. These initial group sizes are generally inadequate, as it is difficult to coordinate the activity of 34 individuals and the operation of dyads within this larger group is not likely to provide the satisfactions that an individual generally derives from group membership. Furthermore, it is less likely that either of these initial corridor groups will congeal into a unit, as the pressures of social density may disrupt this process. Questionnaire data indicate that these assumptions are valid; suite residents report a greater tendency toward solution of problems as a group, while corridor residents report individualistic strategies, and indications of group formation, such as perceived similarity, the degree to which individuals are certain of how their neighbors feel about them, and their willingness to share information about themselves with their neighbors, were found among suite residents, but were not reported by residents of the corridor-design dormitories (see Table 1). These findings suggest that groups do not form as readily in the corridor-style housing. While residents of the suite buildings seem to form residential groups with those living

TABLE 1
Summary of Questionnaire Data Indicating Greater Presence of Group Characteristics Among Suite Residents

	Corridor	Suite	F	p
When you resolve problems, do you do it as a group (1) or individually (7)?	5.131	2.367	55.679	<.001
To what degree do you share the same attitudes with your neighbors? (1-7)[a]	2.905	4.167	14.214	<.001
To what extent do you know how your neighbors regard you as a person? (1-7)[b]	3.135	5.500	38.185	<.001
Number of items residents are willing to disclose to their neighbors (total=10)	4.788	8.810	45.54	<.001

a. 7 = high degree of attitude similarity.
b. 7 = certain of how neighbors regard them.

around them, corridor residents do not appear to participate in proximity-based groups in their residential environments.

CROWDING AND GROUP CONSENSUS

The effects of group formation in these two residential environments were studied by examining the ability of residents to reach agreement on a group consensus task. If groups do not form as readily among corridor residents, it is likely that these residents will not be able to reach a high degree of consensus following group discussion of a task when compared with suite residents. Functioning groups exert pressures on individual members to conform to group opinions and norms, and should be characterized by convergence of members' opinions toward the position of the group. Suite residents, who seem to form groups along proximity dimensions, should display this tendency toward consensus; following group discussion of a task, individual members should show greater agreement on task solutions than corridor residents, who are not active in local residential groups.

In order to test this hypothesis, lists of freshmen residents of both dormitory designs were studied, and 24 four-person experimental groups were assembled. The composition of each group was determined randomly with two important exceptions: (1) half of the groups were composed of corridor residents while the other half were drawn from suite housing, and (2) half of the groups were composed of students living on different floors of a dormitory, while the other half were composed of students who lived across the floor or next door to each other in the corridor housing and who shared suites in these dormitories. In this way, residential condition was crossed with proximity in a two-by-two design. Those groups consisting of students living on various floors were considered to be unaffiliated, while those consisting of neighbors or suitemates were viewed as affiliated groups. Members of each experimental group were reached by telephone and instructed to meet in a neutral lounge for a brief experiment.

After arriving at the lounge, experimental groups were presented the game, "Lost on the Moon" (Hall, 1971). The instructions informed participants that they were to imagine that their spaceship had crash-landed on the dark side of the moon, and that they must now try to reach the mother ship two hundred miles away. The task identified fifteen items (e.g., maps, water) which were available for this expedition, and instructed participants to rank the items in order of their importance for survival. After completing the task individually, participants were asked to discuss the task for twenty minutes and to rank the items as a group. Following this discussion and ranking, each participant again ranked the items individually.

To measure the amount of consensus in each experimental group, individual rankings before and after discussion were combined using the statistic r_{av} (Hare, 1952). The average correlation before discussion reflects the amount of agreement among members of experimental groups on the survival value of each item. The average correlation after discussion, on the other hand, reflects the amount of agreement following discussion and indicates the degree to which each experimental group reached consensus. As can be seen in Table 2, the average amount of agreement before discussion is comparable for all groups, while postdiscussion agreement varies. The comparability of initial agreement was anticipated, as the experimental groups were drawn from among students who are similar with regard to various background characteristics. Among affiliated groups, the average amount of agreement increased significantly after the discussion only for suite groups; suite residents were able to reach more consensus with their suitemates than were corridor residents with their neighbors ($z = 2.58$; $p < .01$). Among unaffiliated experimental groups, consensus was reached by both corridor and suite groups, although suite residents still showed a tendency to reach more agreement after the discussion ($z = 1.43$; $p < .08$).

The data from this experiment indicate that in comparison to suite residents corridor residents are less able to reach agreement following group discussion of a task. Although corridor residents interacting with strangers were able to reach greater consensus relative to prediscussion agreement, suite residents achieved a higher degree of agreement regardless of condition. These findings suggest that corridor residents do not participate in residential groups as do suite residents, and that the relative absence of such groups prevents social structuring that might mitigate the experience of crowding. It appears that the existence of suite-defined groups predisposes suite residents to cooperate more in a group situation, as previous research has

TABLE 2
Average Amount of Agreement Before and After Group Discussion of the Task (unit of analysis = experimental group)

Residential Group	Affiliated Groups			Unaffiliated Groups		
	r_{av} Before	r_{av} After	Change	r_{av} Before	r_{av} After	Change
Corridor	.54	.62	.08	.45	.67	.22
Suite	.59	.86	.27	.52	.85	.33
p	$< .4$	$< .01$	$< .01$	$< .4$	$< .08$	$< .08$

failed to identify any significant population differences between suite and corridor residents. Data collected over the past three years have indicated that these populations are comparable on a number of background dimensions, including personality ratings (using the Omnibus Personality Inventory), family size, ordinal position, Scholastic Aptitude Test scores, residential history, occupational and academic interests, reasons for living in particular campus buildings, and socioeconomic status. Thus, it appears that corridor residents are less able to reach group consensus than suite residents as a function of different levels of social involvement fostered by the dormitory environments.

GROUP MEDIATION OF CROWDING

These considerations suggest that if groups were active in the crowded corridor environments, the quality of life there would be different. The existence of functioning and cohesive groups in these environments would provide residents with some control over their social experience and would provide them with structures similar to those available to suite residents. Although freshmen have little opportunity to structure their floors by arranging to have friends, acquaintances, and pre-established groups move into a particular area, sophomores have this opportunity. By the second year of dormitory residence, students can arrange to have certain people move into certain rooms and to have preestablished groups share parts of or entire residence floors. Such social structuring by dormitory residents should facilitate the formation of cohesive groups in the corridor-design buildings, and should influence, as a result, the nature of crowding experienced in these settings.

A second study was concerned with the effects of group formation among sophomore residents of these dormitories. Attempts to structure one's floor in the corridor dormitories should reflect the need to establish social order; as a result, these attempts should be more pervasive among corridor residents. In addition, the effects of group formation should be more noticeable in the corridor environments, as the need for social order is greater and the interior design furnishes less control than in the suite dormitories. As a result, it was predicted that group cohesion among corridor residents would be related to the experience of crowding; as groups provide social control, the effects of high social density should be reduced and crowding alleviated. However, suite residents generally do not report experiencing crowding at all, and should not experience crowding regardless of the degree to which groups evolve. This also suggests that the degree of experienced crowding in the corridor dormitories should remain greater than that among suite residents, as those who do not belong to groups in the corridor dormitories will still experience crowding as did freshmen. Suite residents who are not members of a group remain protected from interaction by the nature of the interior design of their residential environment.

These phenomena were examined by interviewing 25 residents of the suite dormitories and 37 residents of the corridor dormitories. All students surveyed were sophomores who had lived in corridor-design facilities during their first year on campus, and care was taken to sample residents of as many different floors and dormitory buildings as was possible. With these exceptions, selection of subject was random. Although we have no direct evidence of the comparability of these samples, consistent indications of initial comparability among freshmen residents of these dormitories suggest that these students are similar to one another along a number of dimensions.

Students interviewed were asked a number of questions regarding how much social structure they had attempted to impose in their dormitories, the degree to which these attempts at establishing cohesive groups succeeded, and the degree to which students perceived their dormitory floor as crowded and behaved by avoiding others. When considering each question, subjects were presented with statements which could be used to characterize their residences with reference to each item. These statements were arranged in ascending order, and students were asked to select as many of these statements as possible which accurately described their dormitories. From these responses scores were compiled reflecting the degree of structure, cohesiveness, and crowding perceived by each subject, with higher scores reflecting a greater degree of the dimension under consideration.

It was predicted that corridor residents, recognizing the greater need for social order in their environments, would be more actively engaged in social structuring of their dormitories than would suite residents. This expectation was confirmed; corridor residents reported more attempts to have friends live near them on their floors ($\overline{X}$ = 7.95) than did suite residents ($\overline{X}$ = 4.72; total possible = 16), (t = 2.26; p < .05). In addition, residents of the corridor-design dormitories were more likely to feel that their floor was crowded, that they would like to avoid others there, and that they had difficulty dealing with all of the others on their floor (see Table 3).

When considered alone, corridor residents indicate a strong relationship between perceived group cohesion and crowding (r = −.631; p < .001), while suite residents indicate a substantially weaker relationship (r = −.316; p < .075). Although the difference between these two correlations only approaches significance (z = 1.50; p < .07), it does seem that cohesiveness is not as active in the determination of crowding among suite

TABLE 3
Percentage of Residents of Corridor and Suite Dormitories Indicating Awareness of Crowding and Social Overload on their Dormitory Floor

	Crowded	Avoid Others	Cannot Deal with All Others
Corridor	52	44	41
Suite	4	16	17
x^2	16.7	5.067	3.869
p	<.001	<.05	<.05

(df=1)

residents. As predicted, the weakness of this relationship among suite residents appears to be caused by the fact that few suite residents experience crowding at all. While over half of those corridor residents sampled indicated that they experienced crowding, only one suite resident indicated awareness of such an experience.

Further evidence of the strength of the relationship between cohesiveness of groups and the experience of crowding among corridor residents is summarized in Table 4. Of those residents who perceived their floor as being relatively cohesive, only 19% felt that their floor was crowded, while 76% of those indicating that their floor was not cohesive reported experiencing crowding. Corridor residents who did not indicate the presence of cohesive residential groups on their floors were more likely to feel crowded than those who did report group cohesion in their residential environments (X^2 = 11.98; p < .001).

These findings strongly suggest that the more an individual's social environment is characterized by the presence of a cohesive group, the less crowding and social overload are experienced. The social channels and spatial conventions established by groups provide protection for group members from unwanted outside stimulation and interference, and each individual's control over his social experience is reinforced by the regulatory systems operating within the group. As a result, the presence of a functioning group will mitigate some of the conditions generally preceding the arousal of crowding, and will

TABLE 4
Number of Corridor Residents Indicating that Their Dormitory Floor
Was Crowded by the Degree of Perceived Cohesion on the Floor

	Cohesive	Not Cohesive
Crowded	3	16
Not crowded	13	5

reduce the likelihood that an individual group member will experience crowding or will avoid others. Those sophomores who were able to form groups on their dormitory floor did not experience crowding in the corridor buildings, while those who did not participate in residential groups did experience crowding, much like freshmen residents of these dormitories.

SUMMARY AND CONCLUSIONS

We have presented data that support the notion that functioning groups mediate the experience of crowding and reduce the impact of those conditions which generate crowding stress. Corridor residents are less apt to participate in local residential groups, and are less able to reach group consensus when working with others on a group task. Suite residents, on the other hand, are disposed to participate in local residential groups, primarily within their suite units, and are more able to reach consensus with others. Additional data suggest that sophomore residents of the corridor dormitories are more involved in attempts to have friends and preestablished groups live on their floors than are suite residents, and that the success of these attempts, conceptualized as floor group cohesion, is inversely related to the incidence of crowding and overload. Finally, further evidence of differential levels of perceived crowding in these environments was obtained; corridor residents are more likely to feel that their floor is crowded, that there are too many others with whom they must deal, and that there are others whom they would prefer to avoid.

As with most research of this kind, these findings have implications for the design of social environments. Buildings intended to house large numbers of residents will typically do so at relatively high levels of density, and should be considered in terms of the degree to which their designs facilitate the formation of cohesive residential groups. As the evolution of cohesive groups appears to negate some of the consequences of high density, such consideration should enable designers to create environments which provide structures necessary to reduce the impact of high density. Our data suggest that high social density is associated with the experience of crowding, and that crowding is most often experienced when groups are not present. As it appears unlikely that the world's population growth will slow appreciably, it becomes increasingly more important to acknowledge the inevitability of high density life in the future and to plan our environments in ways which will help ruduce the consequences of these conditions. Although various social, physical, and personal events have already been identified as mediating elements and others will be reported by future research, our study of residential environments suggests that the formation of cohesive groups in these environments is of enormous importance. Residential designs which facilitate group formation will help to reduce the probability that crowding will be experienced.

REFERENCES

BAUM, A. and S. VALINS (1973) "Residential environments, group size, and crowding." Proceedings of the Amer. Psych. Assn.: 211-212.

BAUM, A. and G. DAVIS (forthcoming) "Spatial and social aspects of crowding perception." Environment and Behavior.

COZBY, P. (1973) "Effects of density, activity, and personality on environmental preferences." J. of Research in Personality 7: 45-60.

DESOR, J. (1972) "Toward a psychological theory of crowding." J. of Personality and Social Psychology 21: 79-83.

DOOLEY, B. (1974) "Crowding stress: the effects of social density on men with close or far personal space." Ph.D. dissertation. University of California, Los Angeles.

HALL, E. T. (1966) The Hidden Dimension. New York: Doubleday.

HALL, J. (1971) "Decisions, decisions, decisions." Psychology Today (November).

HARE, A. (1952) "A study of interaction and consensus in different sized groups." Amer. Soc. Rev. 17: 261-267.

SAEGERT, S. (1973) "Crowding: cognitive overload and behavioral constraint." Proceedings of the EDRA IV conference.

SCHOPLER, J. and M. WALTON (1974) "The effects of expected structure, expected enjoyment, and participants internality-externality upon feelings of being crowded." University of North Carolina. (unpublished)

STOKOLS, D. (1972) "A social-psychological model of human crowding phenomena." J. of the Amer. Institute of Planners 38: 72-83.

VALINS, S. and A. BAUM (1973) "Residential group size, social interaction, and crowding." Environment and Behavior 5: 421-439.

ROOM SIZE, GROUP SIZE, AND DENSITY
Behavior Patterns in a Children's Psychiatric Facility

MAXINE WOLFE *is an Assistant Professor in the Environmental Psychology Program at the Graduate Center of the City University of New York. In addition to the continuing study of the children's hospital, she is involved in research on privacy and research on the design and evaluation of day-care centers.*

For the past five years we have been studying the relationship between the physical design of a children's psychiatric hospital and the patterns of behavior and use of space that evolved over time (Wolfe and Rivlin, 1972; Rivlin and Wolfe, 1972; Rivlin et al., 1973). The present paper draws on data collected in these studies. It focuses on the use of bedrooms and particularly, on the relationship between room size, group size, density, and predominant patterns of behavior.

In the literature on design of psychiatric facilities (Bayes, 1967; Bayes and Francklin, 1971; Bettelheim, 1974; Ittelson et al., 1970) "bedroom size" usually refers to two separate aspects: the number of people assigned to a bedroom (group size) and the actual total square footage of the bedroom (room size). In architectural space programs, as in the case of the children's hospital we studied, a given amount of square feet is allotted to living areas and there is a minimum number of

AUTHOR'S NOTE: *This study was supported by Research Grants MH 18010-01 through 18010-05 from the National Institute of Mental Health. The author would like to thank Leanne Rivlin, Arza Churchman, Marian Beyda, Linda Lewin, Alan Sommerman, Richard Olsen, and Wally Wentworth for their help in data collection and John Best for his help in programming and data analysis.*

square feet per child per bedroom (density). Most often the total amount of space in a bedroom increases in proportion to the number of children the room is designed to accommodate. Thus, density remains relatively the same while both number and room size vary.

Each of these aspects of bedroom size (number, space, and density) may have different effects on the frequency of use of bedrooms and on the patterns of behavior occurring in bedrooms when they are used. The only research in this area, however, is the work of Ittelson, Proshansky, and Rivlin (1970a). They found that the type and range of activities in bedrooms in adult psychiatric facilities were related to the *number of persons assigned* to the bedrooms (potential group size). While almost all bedrooms functioned as private rooms— only one patient used a bedroom at one time (actual group size)—single person bedrooms showed the widest range of activities. Increasing the number of persons assigned increased the amount of isolated passive behavior (sleeping, lying awake, sitting alone). Thus, while actual group size during use was the same in all bedrooms, potential group size varied and affected the behavior patterns. A single person bedroom seemed to provide the patient with more freedom of choice in what he/she did in the room, probably because the possibility of intrusion was lowered and the room was actually perceived to be "private."

Ittelson et al. (1970a) did not consider room size or density. In addition, their research focused on adult patients. In an earlier study (Rivlin et al., 1973) we found that although all of the children's bedrooms functioned mainly as places for isolated passive behavior, the total amount of such behavior was lower for the younger children as compared to the adolescents. Furthermore, research has shown that for normal children the definition of privacy as "aloneness" becomes more salient with increasing age (Wolfe and Laufer, 1974). Younger children may experience physical aloneness as more frightening than freeing. Thus, differing group sizes may be related to very different patterns of behavior in children as compared to adults.

The use of bedrooms in children's psychiatric facilities as a function of group size, room size, and density has not been investigated previously. Bayes (1967) and Bayes and Francklin (1971) treat room size and group size as separate issues, but do not mention density. In relation to room and group size, the opinions of several psychiatrists are cited, including the opinion that too large a room can produce anti-social behavior, but no empirical evidence is presented. Bettelheim (1974), on the basis of his experience in the Orthogenic School, believes that: (1) private rooms create anxiety for disturbed children because they symbolize too much independence and self-reliance, and (2) children in two-person bedrooms become too emotionally dependent on one another: if they are both together they are afraid to offend one another by leaving or not interacting; if a visitor is with one child, the other child does not know whether to stay or leave. Bettelheim advised that six to eight children in a room is an ideal number, allowing fourteen to sixteen square yards for private use. These ideas are not supported with specific data.

While research on bedroom size has been limited, research on the general issue of density is available and is reviewed in detail elsewhere in this issue. The main point of this literature for our purposes is that behavior is influenced more by the manner in which given levels of density are achieved than by the level of density itself. Children in nursery school settings move closer to one another (McGrew, 1970) and will show less aggressive behavior (Loo, 1972) when density is created by decreasing the total space available while maintaining a constant group size. On the other hand, they will maintain physical distance from one another (McGrew, 1970) and show increased aggression and decreased social interaction (Hutt and Vaizey, 1966) when group size is increased, but the total amount of space remains constant. Thus, the effects of space and number can be different.

In contrast to the above mentioned density studies and to most studies of group size (Thomas and Fink, 1963), we attempted to look at issues of room size, group size, and density as they occurred naturally within the context of an ongoing social and physical environment—a children's psychiatric institution—and, more specifically, within a certain part of that environment, the children's bedrooms.

Although each bedroom in the living units (apartments) of the hospital was designed for a specified number of children and the total amount of space increased with designated group size, frequently the actual assignment was not to capacity. One child could be in a one-bed, two-bed, or four-bed room; two children might be assigned to a two-bed or a four-bed room. Thus, it would appear that we had naturally occurring combinations of space, number, and density. However, in our earlier studies, we found that, in the children's living areas, 80% of all activities were one-person activities; only 11% were two-person activities, and the remainder were three- or four-person activities (Rivlin et al., 1973). This occurred in spite of the existence of spaces that were designed for groups ranging in size from 1 to 24. Furthermore, even though the actual number of children assigned to a bedroom ranged from 1 to 4, our initial analysis of the bedroom data reported here indicated that the average number of children in a bedroom at any one time was 1.10. Thus, we found that any analysis of bedroom use would have to be in terms of potential group size and potential density.

We did have reason to suspect that the bedrooms, or any environment for that matter, would be used differently when potential group size and potential density varied. The work of Ittelson et al., (1970a), described earlier, indicated that potential group size was a factor affecting bedroom use. Furthermore, we reasoned that potential number and potential density are psychological components of all naturally occurring, stable environments. Behavior patterns and use of space in normal daily living environments (home, office, and school) are based on our past experience in these environments and on our expectations about what will or can occur in these environments. If, for example, we are seeking a place to be alone, we may choose a place we know will not be potentially available to others. If we are seeking a place for intimate conversation, we may eliminate places where the presence of others or the physical closeness of others will lower the possibility of achieving our goal. The children's hospital is no different in these respects. Patterns of use have evolved over time (Wolfe and Rivlin, 1972; Rivlin and Wolfe, 1972), and the patterns we see at any one point in time must reflect the expectations of the individuals involved.

Within the context of institutional life, where most of the day is spent in programmed activities and in spaces shared by all of the children, the bedroom is the child's only personal space. Yet the room may not belong to only one child. Usually, the sharing of a bedroom by two children is seen as a way of promoting interaction and intimate relationships. However, the sharing of a bedroom by children who have difficulty in interpersonal relationships, within the context of entire days of programmed interaction, may create more withdrawal than interaction. In fact, in the one study comparing the effects of increased number on the behavior of disturbed and normal children, Hutt and Vaizey (1966) found that while normal children remained in the center of the group and became more aggressive, autistic children withdrew to the periphery of the room and sought support from the adults present. Thus, the number of children sharing a bedroom may be of particular importance in terms of the child's perception of his/her ability to use it as a place for retreat, withdrawal, or intimate social relationships.

When dealing with institutionalized children, the size of a bedroom space may be as important as the size of the bedroom group. When a child is sole occupant of a bedroom, does the size of that room make a difference in the child's use of the room? We suspected that a larger room might be frightening and used less often than a smaller room which could provide more physical and, hence, psychological security.

It seemed more likely that space and number might interact in determining use of bedrooms. For children who have difficulty in interpersonal relationships, sharing a small room with another child might require more interpersonal coordination of activity than the children are capable of, and each child may use the room less as a way of avoiding this difficulty. In a larger room, the presence of a second child might require less coordination of activity, and hence, each child might use it more.

Some of the bedrooms were assigned to capacity (one child in a one-bed room, two in a two-bed room, four in a four-bed room). In these naturally occurring instances, the density in each bedroom was approximately the same, because total space and number of children increased proportionately. Yet, we suspected that we would find different patterns of behavior in these rooms because of the different meaning of each of these situations to the children involved. The one-child, one-bed room is clearly the most private; the two-child, two-bed room would seem to create the most emotional dependence (Bettelheim, 1974) and, hence, necessitate the most coordination of activity; the four-child, four-bed room has less privacy, but each child is less emotionally dependent on each of the other children. Thus, we suspected that the psychological aspects of space and number would produce the greatest use of the one-child, one-bed room and least use in the two-child, two-bed room.

These speculations reflect the complexity of factors which we believed might affect the use of bedrooms. In the research reported here, we have attempted to clarify the role of some of these factors. We hope to add to the general information concerning the behavioral effects of room size, group size, and density, as well as to provide information which would aid in decision-making to those involved in the planning, design, and administration of residential psychiatric facilities for children.

SETTING

The children's psychiatric hospital is a state facility designed to provide inpatient care for children ranging in age from 6 to 16. It has residence facilities, as well as a school, areas for occupational therapy, recreation, diagnosis, and treatment. The building is divided into 4 areas: a living area, a recreational area, an administrative area, and a school area. Eight houses, or ward units, arranged in 4 pairs, one above the other, provide residence facilities for 24 children each. The house consists of a central corridor leading off to a dayroom with a kitchenette, a nurses' station with an adjacent bench area, a laundry room, a seclusion room, and three apartments called "living units." Each living unit has an entry foyer leading to its own living room and four bedrooms, two single-bed rooms, one two-bed room, and a four-bed room.

DESCRIPTION OF THE CHILDREN

The hospital has programs for both full-care (sleep-in) and day-care children. Since day-care children did not have assigned bedroom space and were rarely in the living units, the data presented represent the full-care children only. Over the four studies, there were sixty full-care children, ranging in age from eight to sixteen. Half of these children were between eight and twelve years of age; the other half were thirteen to sixteen. In the first three studies only one of the eight houses was occupied; in the fourth study, two houses were occupied. In the first three studies, the children's living units were not age segregated; in the fourth study each age group lived in a separate house. The children were almost all diagnosed as having "behavior disorders" with the primary symptoms of "acting out" and/or "impulsive behavior." Only one or two of the children were diagnosed as "childhood schizophrenics." Some children were receiving medication; others were not.

BEDROOMS

There were three different size bedrooms in each living unit, and at the time of these studies, none of the bedrooms had doors. The smallest, designated as a one-bed room, measured 76.02 square feet; the designated two-bed room measured 171.04 square feet; and the designated four-bed room measured 326.98 square feet. Each bedroom had enough furniture for the designated number of occupants (1 to 4) even when less children were assigned. There was a bed (7' x 3') and a storage unit (6' x 3' x 22") for each child. In the designated two- and four-bed rooms, it was usual for the storage unit to be attached to the headboard (creating a "personal area"). In the single-bed rooms, the storage unit fit into a recess in one wall. Each bedroom had one table, the one in the single-bed room being somewhat smaller. The beds in all of the rooms were usually placed against a wall. If we account for the furniture present in each of these rooms, the actual amount of free floor space was 49.52 square feet, 118.05 square feet, and 220.99 square feet in the one-, two-, and four-bed rooms, respectively.

GROUP SIZE

The number of children assigned to a bedroom did not always match the designated number. The one-bed room always had only one child assigned; the two-bed rooms had either one, two, or three children assigned; and the four-bed rooms had from one to four children actually assigned. Assignment to a bedroom was made on a random basis. The child had no choice in assignment and a new child was assigned to whichever room was not fully occupied. However, a one-bed room was always assigned first if a choice was available between that and a multiple occupancy room.

POTENTIAL DENSITY

The actual amount of free floor space available per assigned occupant varied from 29.01 square feet (three children occupying a designated two-bed room) to 220.99 square feet (one child in a designated four-bed room). Table 1 indicates the range of square footage/person which occurred naturally during our studies. It should be noted that these density figures represent the potential density, i.e., if all children assigned were in the room at one time. We will not present data for the two-bed, three-person room or the four-bed, three-person, since each is represented by only one bedroom in one study.

TABLE 1
Potential Density as a Function of Varying Room Size
and Potential Group Size

| | | Room Size and Designated Occupancy | | |
		One Bed (49.52 ft.^{2})	Two Beds (118.05 ft.^{2})	Four Beds (220.99 ft.^{2})
Potential Group Size:	1 child	49.52 (20)[a]	118.05 (7)	220.99 (4)
Number of Children	2 children	—[b]	59.02 (7)	110.50 (5)
Assigned	3 children	—	29.01 (1)[c]	73.66 (1)
	4 children	—	—	55.25 (6)

a. The number in parentheses represents the number of bedrooms in this category over all four studies.
b. These combinations never occurred.
c. An additional bed and storage unit were moved in.

METHOD AND PROCEDURE

In order to study the use of space in the hospital, a series of four observational studies were conducted, covering two and one-half years of the hospital's functioning. Data for the present paper were obtained by combining bedroom-use data from all four studies.

The basic approach in quantifying and describing behavior patterns and the use of the bedrooms was the behavioral mapping technique (Ittelson et al., 1970b). This standardized observational method, developed in previous studies, provides a profile of all activities observed, the participants, the time of the activity, and specific location. Trained observers record activities into 69 coded behaviors which, for the purposes of data analysis, are combined into 19 analytic categories. These categories are: (1) aggression; (2) high-energy physical release; (3) high-energy organized; (4) high-energy unorganized; (5) low-energy organized; (6) isolated active; (7) isolated passive; (8) domestic; (9) media; (10) music; (11) orientation; (12) meetings; (13) exploration; (14) cuddling—holding a child; (15) idiosyncratic behavior; (16) talking; (17) telephoning; (18) traffic; and (19) miscellaneous (see Rivlin and Wolfe, 1972, for a complete description of the categories).

Data were obtained by having an observer make a predetermined tour every fifteen minutes, covering all areas of each house. For each room or area, the observer recorded ongoing activity, the number, residence status (full or day care) and sex of patients, and the number of staff present. Observations were made throughout the active periods of the day: from 10 to 12 and 1 to 4 p.m. and 6 to 9 p.m. Observation was done only on the weekdays, since most of the children went home for the weekend.

Over the four studies there were a total of 25 days of observation with a total of eight hours of observation per day Monday through Thursday, and five hours on Friday, since most children went home for the weekend at 5 p.m.

RESULTS

BEDROOM USE

Bedroom use was evaluated by three criteria: the percentage of occupied observation periods; the average number of children present when the rooms were occupied; and the percentage of room use per child. Before examining bedroom use as a function of room size, group size, and density, we must reiterate the general pattern of bedroom use described in the introduction. Combining all rooms over all days of observation there were 5,951 separate observation periods and in only 776 (13.03%) of these was the bedroom occupied (a room was counted as being occupied as long as at least one child was present). In an earlier study (Rivlin and Wolfe, 1972) we found that only approximately 26% of the activity in the entire hospital took place in the house areas, while 74% occurred in other areas of the hospital. It is not surprising then, that the bedrooms were occupied so infrequently. During the 776 occupied observations, a total of 854 children were observed in 781 activities. Thus, the mean number of children in a bedroom at any one time was 1.10, and the mean number involved in any activity was 1.09. All of the bedrooms, at any one moment in time, were functioning as predominantly one-person rooms.

Table 2 shows the percentage of occupied observation periods, the average number of children present per occupied observation, and the percentage of room use per child as a function of room size, potential group size, and potential density. The percentage of occupied observation periods was not significantly related to room size, nor was it related to potential density (r_s = −.71, n = 6, p = N.S.). It was directly related, however, to the number of children assigned (potential group size). The percentage of occupied observation periods was 25.52%, 13.75%, and 11.26% for the four-person, two-person, and one-person bedrooms, respectively.

The number of children present during an occupied observation also increases with the number of children assigned. The average number of children present during an occupied observation period was 1.026, 1.109, and 1.352 for the one-person, two-person and four-person bedroom. However, examining the number of children present as a function of number of children who could potentially use it, we find that the two- and four-person bedrooms have less than their assigned number present at any one time (55.4% and 33.8%), while the one-person bedroom has more than its assigned number (102.6%).

Another way to look at bedroom use is to determine the percentage of room use per assigned child (percentage of room use per assigned child equals percent occupied observation periods times number of children observed per occupied observation/number of children assigned; see Table 2, line C and Figure 1). Percentage of room use per child is not directly related to potential density (r_s = .31, n = 6, p = N.S.). The data revealed that the children using their rooms most were in a one-person, one-bed room. Z-tests (Edwards, 1960) of the significance of the difference between proportions reveal that when one child is assigned, that child uses a one-bed room somewhat more than a two-bed room (12.42% versus 10.32%, z = 1.62, p = .10) and significantly more than a four-bed room (12.42% versus 7.78%;

TABLE 2
Bedroom Use as a Function of Room Size, Potential Group Size, and Potential Density

	One Bed (49.52 ft.²)	Two Beds (118.05 ft.²)		Four Beds (220.99 ft.²)		
Potential group size[a]	1	1	2	1	2	4
Potential density[a] (ft.²)	49.52	118.05	59.02	220.99	110.50	55.25
A. % Occupied observation periods	12.18%	9.38%	10.45%	7.78%	18.82%	25.52%
B. Average number of children present	1.02	1.10	1.11	1.00	1.11	1.35
C. % Room use per child	12.42%	10.32%	5.85%	7.78%	10.44%	8.61%
Number of observation periods	2,931	757	854	360	542	507
Number of Bedrooms	20	7	7	4	5	6

a. Potential group size refers to the number of children sharing the bedroom; potential density refers to the ft.²/person if all children were in the room together.
b. Based on total number of observation periods.

$z = 2.61$, $p = .009$). The level of use of the four-bed room is lower than for the two-bed room, but not significantly (10.32% versus 7.78%, $z = 1.41$, $p = .16$). Thus increasing the total amount of space, when only one child is assigned, results in decreased bedroom use by the child. When the potential group size is two, i.e., when two children are sharing a bedroom, increasing the total space available increases each child's use of the room ($z = 2.23$, $p = .026$).

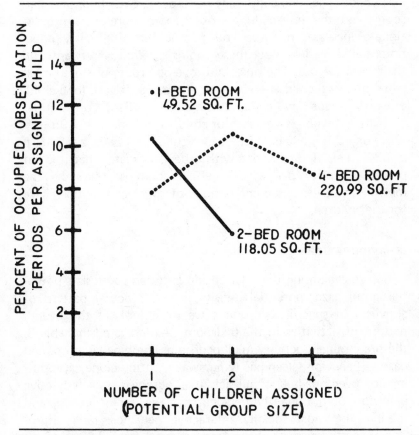

Figure 1: Percentage of Room Use Per Assigned Child as a Function of Room Size and Potential Group Size.

If we examine the data in terms of increasing number, we find that in a small room (two-bed room, 118.05 square feet), increasing the number of children assigned significantly decreases each child's use (10.32% versus 5.95%, $z = 2.64$, $p = .008$). In a larger room (220.99 square feet), the percentage of use varies less with increasing number (one child versus two children, $z = 1.34$, $p = .18$; one child versus four children, $z < 1$; two children versus four children, $z = 1.02$, $p = .30$), and was maximal for each child when two children were assigned.

One further point in relation to the percentage of room use per child. The one-child, one-bed room; two-child, two-bed room; and the four-child, four-bed room represent a proportionate increase in space and number creating fairly equal potential densities. Yet, these rooms differed significantly in their levels of use. The one-child, one-bed room was used most while the two-child, two-bed room was used least (one-child, one-bed versus two-child, two-bed, $z = 5.43$, $p < .001$; two-child, two-beds versus four-child, four-beds, $z = 1.95$, $p = .051$; one-child, one-bed versus four-child, four-beds, $z = 2.45$, $p = .034$). This finding, along with others, indicates that it is not potential density, per se, which affects room use, but rather the meaning that various combinations of space and number have for the children.

BEHAVIOR PATTERNS

Before evaluating the relationship between room size, potential group size, potential density, and the actual pattern of activities in specific bedrooms, we must look at the overall pattern of activities in the bedrooms. As indicated in Table 3, the predominant activity in all bedrooms combined was isolated passive behavior (sleeping, lying awake, sitting alone) accounting for over one-half of all activities observed. Isolated active behavior, predominantly personal hygiene, ranks second, and talking, the most socially interactive behavior, ranks third. Together, these three behaviors account for 82.33% of all behavior in the bedroom. Our analysis, then, will focus on these

TABLE 3
Frequency and Percentage of Children's
Activities Within all Bedrooms[a]

Activity Category	f	%
Isolated Passive[b]	438	56.08
Isolated Active[b]	107	13.70
Talking[b]	98	12.55
High-Energy Unorganized	24	3.07
Low-Energy Organized	16	2.05
Domestic	14	1.79
Aggression	13	1.66
Media	13	1.66
Traffic	12	1.54
Idiosyncratic Behavior	11	1.41
Explore	6	.77
High-Energy Physical Release	4	.51
Orientation	3	.38
Music	2	.25
High-Energy Organized	2	.25
Cuddle-Hold	1	.13
Miscellaneous	17	2.18
Total Number of Activities Observed	781	100.00%
Total Number Participants	854	
Total Number of Occupied Observation Periods	776	
Total Number of Observation Periods	5,951	

a. Treating the bedrooms in each study as separate rooms, the total number of bedrooms observed over the four studies was 49.
b. Isolated passive behavior included crying alone, lying awake, sitting alone, sleeping, standing alone, looking out a window alone.
Isolated active behavior was predominantly personal hygiene, i.e., combing hair, dressing or undressing, and so forth.
Talking involved any conversation which appeared to be the predominant activity even when other activities were involved.

three behavior categories as a function of room size, potential group size, and potential density (see Table 4 and Figure 2).

A Spearman rank correlation (Siegel, 1956) was computed between percentage of activity observed and potential density. Each room size and group size combination was assigned a rank from one to six depending on the resultant density (220.99 square feet/person = 1; 49.52 square feet/person = 6) and the

TABLE 4

Percentage of Isolated Passive, Isolated Active, and Talking Activity in the Bedrooms

	One-Bed Room (49.52 ft.^{2})	Two-Bed Room (118.05 ft.^{2})			Four-Bed Room (220.99 ft.^{2})	
		(A)	(B)	(C)	(D)	
Potential Group Size	1	1	2	1	2	4
Potential density (ft.^{2})	49.52	118.05	59.02	220.99	110.50	55.25
$\bar{X}$ Percentage of Isolated Passive[a]	57.49	40.12	26.11	31.06	63.86	58.06
$\bar{X}$ Percentage of Talking[a]	12.76	26.44	16.56	33.77	3.38	12.25
$\bar{X}$ Percentage of Isolated Active	12.10	8.23	23.54	25.00	16.66	14.85
Number of Participants Per Activity	1.05	1.18	1.19	1.04	1.08	1.16
Number of Bedrooms	20	7	7	4	5	6
Total Number of Activities Observed	347	66	84	24	105	155

a. Based on total number of activities observed in that room.

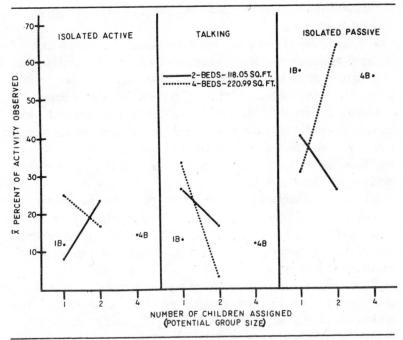

Figure 2: Percentage of Specific Activities Observed as a Function of Room Size and Potential Group Size (one-child, one-bed room [1B] and four-child, four-bed room [4B] not included in analysis of variance).

observed amount of a given behavior (e.g., isolated passive) was ranked from highest to lowest. The observed amounts of isolated passive, talking, and isolated active behaviors were not significantly correlated with potential density (r_s = −.314 for isolated passive; −.67 for talking; and +.62 for isolated active behavior, n = 6, p = N.S.).

The experimental design created by naturalistic conditions did not permit an application of analysis of variance to all of these data. However, by taking a portion of the data, we created a two-by-two design varying room size (two bed and four bed) and group size (one child and two children). The use of analysis of variance on this portion of the data enables us to perform a more stringent test of the effects of room size and potential group size on the percentage of specific behaviors (isolated passive, isolated active, talking) observed in rooms varying in these conditions. Table 4 (columns A, B, C, and D) and Figure 2 present these data.

An analysis of variance indicates that the percentage of isolated active behavior (predominantly personal hygiene) was not significantly related to either room size, potential group size, or the interaction of these variables. Z-tests indicate that the amount of isolated active behavior in the two-bed room increases significantly when a second child is assigned (one child = 8.23%, two children = 23.54%; $z = 7.89$; $p < .001$), while in the four-bed room the decrease with the addition of a second child is not significant ($z < 1$).

An analysis of variance indicates that the percentage of talking observed was related only to the potential group size ($F = 3.53$, df = 1/19; $.10 < p > .05$). Whether in a large or small room, the assignment of a second child results in less use of the room for conversation.

Room size and potential group size tend to interact to affect the amount of isolated passive behavior observed in the bedrooms ($F = 2.8639$, df = 1/19, $p = .11$). In the smaller room adding a person decreases the use of the room for isolated passive behavior ($z = 1.824$, $p = .07$) while in the larger room, the potential presence of another person increases the use of the room for isolated passive behavior ($z = 2.93$, $p = .003$).

Thus, adding a person to the smaller room decreases its use for both social interaction and withdrawal, and its use for personal hygiene increases under these circumstances. In the smaller room, then, the assignment of a second child produces a more even use of the room for all three activities, while with only one occupant assigned isolated passive behaviors predominate.

Another way of evaluating the effects of space and number involves utilizing some data which could not be included in the analysis of variance. First, we can evaluate the effects of increasing space by comparing the observed level of each of the three activities for one child in a one-bed, two-bed, or four-bed room. Second, we can evaluate the effects of increasing number by comparing the observed level of the three activities for the four-bed room when one, two, or four children are assigned.

Increasing space, when one child is assigned to a room, results in less use of the room for isolated passive behaviors. There is significantly less isolated passive behavior observed in the one-child, two-bed room than in the one-child, one-bed room (z = 2.60, p = .009) and somewhat, although not significantly, less in the one-child, four-bed room as compared to the one-child, two-bed room ($z < 1$, p = N.S.). Increased space results in more use of the room for conversation. The amount of talking observed is significantly greater in the one-child, two-bed than in the one-child, one-bed room (z = 2.85, p = .004) and somewhat, although not significantly, greater in the one-child, four-bed than in the one-child, two-bed room ($z < 1$, p = N.S.). The one-child, one-bed room (or "private" room), then, is used significantly more than the larger rooms for isolated passive behavior and less for talking. However, the larger room (four beds) is used significantly more for isolated active behaviors than the two other rooms (four-bed room versus two-bed room, z = 2.11, p = .0348; four-bed room versus one-bed room, z = 1.824, p = .068; two-bed room versus one-bed room, $z < 1$, p = N.S.). Thus, when only one child is assigned, as the amount of space increases, the use of the room becomes more varied because isolated passive behaviors decrease while talking and isolated active behaviors increase.

The analyses of variance enabled us to look at the effects of increasing the number of children assigned from one to two. We can further examine the effects of an increased number of children by comparing the observed level of each type of behavior in the four-bed room when a four-person group is included. We have already shown that, in the four-bed room, as group size increased from one to two children, to amount of isolated behavior increased significantly. We find that the addition of two more children produces a slight, but not significant, decrease in such behavior ($z < 1$, p = N.S.). The amount of isolated active behavior in the four-bed room is not significantly affected by increased group size, either from one to two people or from two to four people. The amount of talking, which decreased significantly when a second child was assigned, increases significantly when two more children are assigned ($z = 2.51$, $p = .012$), but still is significantly less than when only one child is assigned ($z = 4.68$, $p < .01$).

Our final point concerns the effects of equal potential density levels created by proportionate increases of number of children and amount of space. As Table 4 indicates, the one-bed, one-person and four-bed, four-person bedrooms produce roughly the same distribution of activities. These rooms are used predominantly for isolated passive behaviors while talking and isolated active behaviors are observed far less often. The two-child, two-bed room shows no such peaking of isolated passive behaviors. It is used about equally for isolated passive and isolated active behaviors and slightly less for talking. In comparison to the other two rooms, the two-child, two-bed room had a lower use for isolated passive behavior (versus one-child, one-bed room, $z = 5.16$, $p < .001$; versus four-child, four-bed room, $z = 4.72$, $p < .001$) and a higher use for isolated active behaviors (versus one-child, one-bed room, $z = 2.68$, $p = .007$; versus four-child, four-bed room, $z = 1.70$, $p = .09$). Although talking was observed somewhat more often in the two-child, two-bed room, the level of use for this behavior was not significantly different in the one-child, one-bed or four-child, four-bed rooms.

These data again indicate that differences in the patterns of activity are not related to potential density. These differences will have to be explained in terms of the psychological meaning that number and space have for the kinds of behaviors for which bedrooms are used.

DISCUSSION

The present research has differed in several respects from previous density research. The setting was a natural ongoing physical and social environment rather than a transient situation created specifically to study density. We could not manipulate the independent variable of space and number, but had to deal with these variables and their combinations as they were produced by natural factors in the environment. We examined potential density and potential group size rather than "in situ" density and group size. The environment and its inhabitants—a children's psychiatric hospital and "disturbed children"—might be considered special or unusual. Yet, our data support the main point of recent literature on the behavioral effects of density, i.e., *behavior is influenced more by the manner in which given levels of density are achieved than by the level of density itself.*

Potential density, i.e., the number of square feet per person if all people were present, is used in almost all architectural space programming whether for housing or hospitals. Yet, we found that potential density was not related to either bedroom use or behavior patterns. The differences in percentage of room use and patterns of behavior when similar density levels were created by the proportionate increase of space and number (one-child, one-bed room; two-child, two-bed room; four-child, four-bed room) indicate that the *size of space and the number of people are significant, not as parts of a mathematical density factor, but as they interact to create certain psychological density conditions.* In this sense our findings support the views of Loring (1956) and Desor (1972). While our study took place in a children's hospital, we focused, as did Loring (1956), on residential space and as far as we know, as such, it is the only study of the *behavioral* effects of density in a residential setting. It is in these types of settings, whether in or out of hospitals, that issues of privacy, territoriality, and emotional dependence become especially salient.

In the specific context of the children's hospital, and probably in other settings as well, if one is interested in room use on a room efficiency basis, clearly the more children assigned to the room the more often it will be occupied during a given day. But only one child will be in it at any one time and, on an individual basis, each child will use the room less as the assigned number increases. These findings are in agreement with the adult psychiatric hospital studies of Ittelson et al. (1970a).

In terms of the psychological aspects of space and number, the one-child, one-bed room is used most often and clearly is the most private environment. The total space is, by definition, one child's territory (with unambiguous defense rights), and there is total absence of any need for coordinating use or considering use in relationship to another child. Children in a two-child, two-bed room used their rooms least with the four-child, four-bed room falling in between. These latter two rooms differ from the one-child, one-bed room in that they are not private for any of the children assigned and will clearly require territory defense and/or coordination of activity. Why, then, should the two-child, two-bed room be used less often than the four-child, four-bed room?

Thomas and Fink (1963), in their review of the nature of interaction as a function of group size, refer to research (Bales and Borgatta, 1955) which indicated that two-person in situ groups (in comparison to three- to seven-person groups) had unique properties. They showed the lowest rates of overt disagreement and antagonism, but high rates of tension. In their research, subjects could not leave the situation, but we may hypothesize that they would avoid the situation if possible. Bettelheim (1974) has made the same point about two children sharing a bedroom in the Orthogenic School: the emotional dependence of each child on the other made the use of the room uncomfortable. Thus, one reason for the relatively higher use of the four-child, four-bed room is that the two-person group size may have unique properties which support avoidance. However, potential group size is not enough to explain the findings since two children in a four-bed room each used their room more often than two children in a two-bed room. The total amount of space available and its relation to emotional dependence would seem to be critical here. When interpersonal demands (or emotional dependence) are high (i.e., a two-child group), additional space can serve to lessen those demands while less space can heighten them. In a larger space, each child can enter the room without physically confronting the other; their activities can be spatially more separate and dependence can be lessened.

One child's decreasing use of a bedroom as the size of that space increased lends some support to the notion that aloneness in large spaces may be frightening to a child. There is another possible explanation of this finding. Each room, regardless of assigned group size, contained enough bedroom furniture for the designated group size. It is possible, then, that the single child in a two- or four-bed room knew that other children (new admissions) might be assigned. Thus, these rooms were only temporarily private. While the behavior patterns tend to support the former explanation, future research should examine the effects of room size for a private room separate from this confounding factor.

Potential group size and the total amount of space available affected the types of behaviors children engaged in when they were using the bedrooms. Some of our findings are similar to those found for adult patients by Ittelson et al. (1970a). In support of their findings, our study indicated that isolated passive behavior predominated in all of the bedrooms. Similarly, we found that the amount of social behavior (in our study, talking) was related to potential group size. Regardless of the size of the room, the assignment of a second child decreased each child's use of the room for conversation. We can surmise that the possibility of intrusion (having a conversation over-heard) is crucial here. When the potential presence of other people is not the issue, i.e., in a single-person bedroom, then, for the children studied here, the amount of space becomes relevant. Increased space created increased use of the room for talking. If, as we mentioned earlier, a large amount of space is frightening to a child who is alone, then the child may pattern his/her behaviors to make the time in the space less frightening, i.e., invite others in to talk, and engage in active, rather than passive behaviors. This would account for the even distribution of these activities in the one-child, four-bed room.

Contrary to Ittelson et al.'s findings for adult patients, children's use of the bedroom for withdrawal (primarily sleeping) generally decreased with increases in potential group size. The size of the space, an issue they did not consider, influenced the use of rooms for passive behaviors. Increased space resulted in less isolated passive behavior for the child alone, and more isolated behavior when two children shared the space. Children and adolescents, especially those who tend to be hyperactive, may be less capable than adults of screening out unwanted interruptions whether in the form of interpersonal demands or physical stimuli such as noise or visual distraction. As potential group size increases, each child uses the room less as one way of dealing with this problem. But, when possession of a room is shared, a larger amount of space makes it more possible to use the room and to use it for sleeping because the space may lower certain types of stimulation (auditory and visual).

Finally, in contrast to Ittelson et al.'s findings, the child in the private room did not engage in the most evenly distributed range of behaviors. Isolated passive behavior predominated. Developmental differences and/or the difference in the nature of the institutional context for children as compared to adults would seem to account for these contradictory findings. Children have less freedom of choice than adults. This is especially true in children's institutions, as compared to adult institutions, because programmed activities involving many children take up a large part of the day. If we consider aloneness and interaction as balanced needs, the children's institution provides many forced interactive situations and few alone situations. In this hospital especially, it was considered inappropriate for the child to withdraw in situations defined by the program as social. The bedrooms, when they can be used, become the only places considered appropriate for these withdrawal behaviors by the adults in authority. The private room offers the greatest possibility to engage in these behaviors without interruption from other children. Thus, choice does not necessarily have to be reflected by the use of one space for a wide variety of behavior, but may be reflected by the use of certain spaces for specific behaviors which are not possible elsewhere.

DESIGN AND ADMINISTRATIVE IMPLICATIONS

In any specific institution, the type, number, and arrangements of bedrooms must be considered in terms of the specific therapeutic goals of the institution, the overall design of the institution, and the availability of spaces for varieties of activities and types of interactions. However, on the basis of our findings and those of Ittelson et al. (1970a) it seems that:

(1) Potential density should not be the main basis for the allotment of space in residential programming. While a minimum amount of space per person is necessary, it is not sufficient as a basis for design decisions. The total amount of space allotted for particular types of uses must be viewed in terms of the behavior it facilitates or inhibits in a given environment with given group sizes.

(2) Private rooms will be used most often (with the qualification that, if they are too large, they may be frightening and may produce a reactive rather than an active pattern of behavior).

(3) As the number of children assigned to a room increases, the use of the room by each child will decrease and, when used, interactive behaviors will be lowered.

(4) The unique properties of the two-child group seem to require that a two-child bedroom have a larger amount of space than simply double that of a one-child room in order to be viable for each child.

(5) The occurrence of isolated passive behavior in bedrooms is not necessarily negative when viewed in the context of days which are filled with programmed activity taking place in the presence of others. The smaller private room or a substantially larger two-person bedroom would seem to support such behavior under these circumstances.

REFERENCES

BALES, R. F. and E. F. BORGATTA (1955) "Size of group as a factor in the interaction profile," pp. 396-413 in A. D. Hare, E. F. Borgatta, and R. F. Bales (eds.) Small Groups. New York: Alfred A. Knopf.

BAYES, K. (1967) The Therapeutic Effect of Environment on Emotionally Disturbed and Mentally Subnormal Children. Surrey, England: Gresham.

——— and S. FRANCKLIN [eds.] (1971) Designing for the Handicapped. London, England: George Goodwin.

BETTELHEIM, B. (1974) A Home for the Heart. New York: Alfred A. Knopf.

DESOR, J. A. (1972) "Toward a psychological theory of crowding." J. of Personality and Social Psychology 21: 79-83.

EDWARDS, A. (1960) Experimental Design in Psychological Research. New York: Holt, Rinehart & Winston.

HUTT, C. and M. J. VAIZEY (1966) "Differential effects of group density on social behavior." Nature 209: 1371-1372.

ITTELSON, W. H., H. M. PROSHANSKY, and L. G. RIVLIN (1970a) "Bedroom size and social interaction." Environment and Behavior 2: 255-270.

——— (1970b) "The use of behavioral maps in environmental psychology," pp. 658-668 in H. M. Proshansky, W. H. Ittelson, and L. G. Rivlin (eds.) Environmental Psychology: Man and His Physical Setting. New York: Holt, Rinehart & Winston.

LOO, C. M. (1972) "The effects of spatial density on the social behavior of children." J. of Applied Social Psychology 2: 372-381.

LORING, W. C. (1956) "Housing and social problems." Social Problems 3: 160-168.

McGREW, P. L. (1970) "Social and spatial density effects on spacing behavior in preschool children." J. of Child Psychology and Psychiatry 2: 197-205.

RIVLIN, L. G. and M. WOLFE (1972) "The early history of a psychiatric hospital for children. Expectations and reality." Environment and Behavior 4: 33-72.

——— and M. BEYDA (1973) "Age-related differences in the use of space," in W. Prieser (ed.) Environmental Design Research. Stroudsburg, Pa.: Dowden, Hutchinson & Ross.

SIEGEL, S. (1956) Non-parametric Statistics for the Behavioral Sciences. New York: McGraw-Hill.

THOMAS, E. J. and C. F. FINK (1963) "Effects of group size." Psych. Bull. 60: 371-384.

WOLFE, M. and R. S. LAUFER (1974) "The concept of privacy in childhood and adolescence," in S. Margules (ed.) Privacy. Stroudsburg, Pa.: Dowden, Hutchinson & Ross.

WOLFE, M. and L. G. RIVLIN (1972) "Evolution of space utilization patterns in a children's psychiatric hospital," in W. Mitchell (ed.) Environmental Design: Research and Practice: Proceedings of EDRA III Conference. Los Angeles: University of California.

SPATIAL AND PERCEPTUAL COMPONENTS OF CROWDING
Effects on Health and Satisfaction

LARRY M. DEAN *is a Lieutenant, Medical Service Corps. U.S. Navy, and Head, Fleet Problems Branch at the Naval Health Research Center, San Diego.*

WILLIAM M. PUGH *is a Research Psychologist at the Naval Health Research Center, San Diego.*

E. K. ERIC GUNDERSON *is Head, Environmental and Social Medicine Division, at the Naval Health Research Center, San Diego.*

Crowding long has been associated with the rapid spread of infectious disease (Dubos, 1970), and in recent years animal studies and experiments involving human subjects have suggested that crowding may have important social and psychological effects. Animal research seems to be quite clear as to the negative impact of crowding on various animal behaviors (Stokols, 1974; Calhoun, 1962; Christian et al., 1960; Thiessen and Rodgers, 1961). However, the results of research on the effects of crowding in human populations are quite inconsistent. For example, the negative effects of crowding on certain behaviors have been reported by Griffitt and Veitch (1971), while positive effects on related behaviors have been reported by Loo (1972). In addition, some investigators have found no significant relationship between various observed behaviors and crowding (Freedman et al., 1971).

AUTHORS' NOTE: *This is Report 74-55, supported by the Bureau of Medicine and Surgery, Department of the Navy, under Research Work Unit MF51.524.022-0003. Opinions expressed are those of the authors and are not to be construed as necessarily reflecting the official view or endorsement of the Department of the Navy.*

It appears that empirical studies and the integration of results may have been hampered by some confusion in the meaning of the term "crowding." Noting this difficulty, a number of writers (Desor, 1972; Loo, 1973; Stokols, 1972) have called for distinctions between population density as a physical parameter and crowding viewed as a subjective psychological experience. Stokols (1972) distinguished between "density," which referred to physical spatial dimensions, and "crowding" which was defined as a perceptual or experiential response to limited space. Regarding the experiential state of crowding, research has suggested that it may occur as the result of stimulus overload (Desor, 1972; Milgram, 1970; Baum and Valins, 1973), the inability to control adequately interactions with others (Zlutnick and Altman, 1972), perceived restrictions in one's freedom of choice (Proshansky et al., 1970), and/or a disturbance of CNS functioning (Esser, 1973). Underlying each of the above conceptions of crowding is the notion of the individual's perception of density. Therefore, in line with Stokols (1972), it is felt that research needs to focus not only on physical density, but also on the experience of crowding in which individual perceptions are considered.

As part of an earlier study of the effects of shipboard crowding on health, Pugh and Dean (1974) utilized two crowding measures, one reflecting size of physical space and the other, the number of persons in the space. These measures were further separated into two distinct components, a situational component (ship effect) and an individual differences component. These two components were found to have differential validities for predicting illness—illness being better predicted by the situational component.

The purpose of this study was to differentiate further components of crowding and to relate specific crowding components to a variety of behavioral and attitudinal criteria aboard ship, for example: illness and accidents, job satisfaction, and an organizational climate variable.

METHOD

SUBJECTS

Subjects were naval enlisted men aboard thirteen ships, ten of which were minesweepers, one was a destroyer, one was a destroyer-escort, and one was an aircraft carrier. Subjects were requested to fill out a questionnaire, including a section called the Habitability Questionnaire (HQ), which described the crew's living and working conditions aboard ship. A total of 1,200 men were given the questionnaire; 5% of these individuals were dropped from the analyses because of difficulty with the English language or the brevity of their time abord ship. Thus, the final sample included 938 men.

Based on subject's responses to selected HQ items, two measures of crowding were derived which followed the distinction between physical size of an area and the number of people in an area indicated by Stokols (1972) and McGrew (1972). The first, spatial size, was the sum of response values for HQ items referring to the amount of space available in several specific areas (messing area, berthing area, working areas, heads or sanitary facilities, and the ship in general). The second crowding measure was the sum of the response values for the HQ items referring to the number of people occupying the five specific areas enumerated above.

Each crowding measure was divided into three component scores which included situational (ship) and importance components derived in the same manner as in the earlier study (Pugh and Dean, 1974), and a residual component which was the variance remaining when the first components were subtracted from the original crowding scores.

The situational component score was derived by first computing mean crowding scores for each ship, then dividing the thirteen ships into five groups with similar mean scores on each crowding dimension, and finally assigning to each individual the mean crowding scores for his ship group. In the analysis of variance model these values are called main effect or "frequency-weight" scores (Kendall and Stuart, 1966: 12).

Importance scores were derived from two HQ items, one reflecting the importance to the individual of "size of space" and the other reflecting the importance of "number of people in space." Both items were rated on a three-point scale: "not important," "somewhat important," and "very important."

The residual components were derived by subtracting the situational and importance components from the original crowding scores.

The crowding measures and their components were correlated with the following criteria: illness rate, accident rate, job satisfaction, satisfaction with living conditions (habitability satisfaction), intention to stay in the Navy, and perceived interdepartmental cooperation. Illness rates (including accidents) were computed by calculating for each individual the total number of initial dispensary visits during the previous year and dividing this total by the length of time he was aboard. Accident rates were computed separately in a similar manner.

The job satisfaction scale consisted of a composite of three questionnaire items utilized in previous studies (McDonald and Gunderson, 1974). This brief scale was shown to have adequate reliability and to correlate substantially with the Smith Job Descriptive Index (Smith et al., 1969).

The habitability satisfaction scale was based on the item, "Choose the number that most nearly describes how satisfied you are with conditions in general for each of the shipboard areas mentioned below." (These included the five specific areas mentioned earlier.) Responses were given on a five-point scale ranging from "highly dissatisfied" to "highly satisfied," and the response values were summed to provide the habitability satisfaction score.

Another satisfaction criterion, intention to stay in the Navy, was based on the individual's response on a five-point scale, ranging from "definitely want to get out" to "definitely plan to make the Navy . . . a career."

One indicator of organizational climate was included in the analysis. A score reflecting degree of communication and cooperation between divisions of the ship was derived by summing response values for four HQ items: "There is poor communication between divisions aboard this ship" (scaled "strongly agree" to "strongly disagree"); "Most of the divisions are more concerned with their own goals and problems than with the broader goals of the ship" (scaled "strongly agree" to "strongly disagree"); "How much contact do you have with workers outside your division?" (scaled "almost no contact" to "a great deal of contact"); and "Aboard this ship friendly, cooperative relationships exist among the men of different divisions" (scaled "strongly disagree" to "strongly agree").

RESULTS

In the first stage of the analysis, the original crowding scores—space size and number of people—were correlated with the six criterion variables. As can be seen in Table 1, at least one of the original crowding scores correlated significantly ($p < .05$) with each of the criteria; the correlation between the number of people variable and accidents was quite low, but significant.

Crowding not only appeared to have an important effect on overall satisfaction with living conditions (habitability satisfaction), but also relationships with job satisfaction and intention to remain in the Navy were indicated. Crowding also was related to illnesses and accidents. The two crowding measures tended to have similar patterns of correlation with the various criteria, although some minor differences can be noted.

In the next stage of analysis, the three component scores for each crowding measure (ship, importance, and residual) were correlated with the six criteria. As can be seen in Table 2, a more differentiated pattern of relationships emerged when crowding scores were reduced to specific components. Most of the relationship between crowding and general satisfaction with

TABLE 1

Correlations of Crowding Measures with Attitudinal and Behavioral Criteria[a]

Crowding Measures	Dispensary Visits	Accidents	Criterion Variables			
			Job Satisfaction	Stay in Navy	Habitability Satisfaction	Department Cooperation
Space size	12[c]	06	-15[c]	-10[c]	-61[c]	-13[c]
Number of people	11[c]	08[b]	-17[c]	-13[c]	-55[c]	-14[c]
Number of cases	799	799	922	937	938	938

a. Decimals are omitted.
b. p < .05.
c. p < .01.

TABLE 2
Correlations of Components of Crowding Measures with Attitudinal and Behavioral Criteria[a]

Crowding Measures and Components	Dispensary Visits	Accidents	Criterion Variables Job Satisfaction	Stay in Navy	Habitability Satisfaction	Department Cooperation
Space size:						
Ship	14[c]	08[b]	06	04	-24[c]	04
Importance	02	03	-02	00	-21[c]	-03
Residual	06	03	-20[c]	-13[c]	-55[c]	-16[c]
Number of people:						
Ship	15[c]	08[b]	02	-03	-21[c]	-04
Importance	08[b]	04	04	-02	-28[c]	-07[b]
Residual	05	05	-18[c]	-13[c]	-48[c]	-13[c]
Number of cases	799	799	922	937	938	938

a. Decimals are omitted.
b. p < .05.
c. p < .01.

living conditions was accounted for by the residual component, thus indicating that general habitability satisfaction was largely determined by individual differences in perception while the particular ship and the expressed importance of crowding played a relatively minor role. The residual (individual differences) score was the only component that correlated with the job satisfaction and intention to stay in the navy criteria.

With respect to dispensary visits and accidents, the situational (ship) component of crowding was most significant; the importance and residual components of crowding had little or no relationship to illness rates. The separation of crowding into its components helped to clarify specific sources of illness variance and tended to increase the predictability of the illness criterion.

The results for the perceived interdepartmental cooperation criterion also were clarified in Table 2. The residual components of the crowding measures accounted for most of the relationship indicated with the organizational cooperation, thus suggesting that differences in perceptions of interdepartmental cooperation were largely attributable to individual and subgroup differences rather than to situational (ship) differences.

SUMMARY AND DISCUSSION

Crowding is a complex concept which cannot be reduced to purely physical dimensions. Spatial size, numbers of people, and personal needs apparently interact to determine perceptions of crowding and their behavioral consequences. Crew members aboard Navy ships readily responded when asked to rate the degree of crowding in their living and working spaces, and they tended to exhibit consensus in describing crowded conditions on their ships (Pugh and Dean, 1974). When subjects were scored in terms of the consensus of their ship-group (situational component) and in terms of individual deviations from the consensus (importance and residual components), a meaningful pattern of relationships with the criteria emerged. The pattern of correlations obtained was consistent with the notion that the consensus (ship-group) scores reflected actual physical characteristics of the ships (e.g., density), while the difference scores reflected personal values (importance) or other individual and subgroup differences of crew members.

Until recently, the deleterious effects of crowding on health have generally been attributed to increases in infectious diseases in densely populated communities. The present results were consistent with the expectation that general illness rate, which included a substantial proportion of infectious conditions, would be associated with crowding, although the correlation was quite modest ($r = .15$). It is recognized that crowding is only one of many environmental factors that may affect the spread of infectious agents. The simplistic notion that crowding affects disease rate solely by facilitating contagious infection has been challenged by a number of investigators, and a more complex model for the onset of disease is emerging which emphasizes the impact of psychosocial stimuli on physiological responses and the moderating influence of the social environment on susceptibility to disease-producing agents (Cassel, 1971; Gunderson and Rahe, 1974; Kiritz and Moos, 1974).

The satisfaction measures, including intention to remain in the navy, were correlated primarily with the residual components of the crowding measures. This result suggests that there are multiple sources of satisfaction and variations in levels of satisfaction among individuals and subgroups within ships. Thus, crowding had an impact on satisfaction, but apparently more as a function of perceptual differences and presumably individual needs than as a response to the physical environment of the ship itself. Looking at the relationship in another way, one finds that men who were dissatisfied—for whatever reasons—were more likely to rate their living areas as crowded. This same trend was noted by MacDonald and Oden (1973) in another context.

It was apparent that habitability satisfaction, while strongly related to the residual component, was also somewhat affected by the ship and importance components. This seems reasonable in view of the consensus with respect to quality of living conditions that was present for the various ships.

It was of special interest that the organizational climate variable, perceived interdepartmental cooperation, was related primarily to the residual components of the two crowding measures and was not related to ship differences. This result indicates that judgments of interdepartmental cooperation were primarily dependent on individual or subgroup differences in perception rather than reflecting an attribute of the ship as a whole.

The "space size" and "number of people" crowding variables were quite similar in their relationships with the attitudinal and behavioral criteria of this study. It may be advantageous, then, to combine these into a single "perceived crowding" variable which could be used in conjunction with objective measures of physical density, for example, number of square feet of floor space per person in berthing or messing areas. Such measures of "population density" and "perceived crowding" are currently being used in ongoing studies of shipboard environments and should make possible more precise evaluation of the effects of crowding on health, satisfaction, and organizational effectiveness.

REFERENCES

BAUM, A. and S. VALINS (1973) "Residential environments, group size and crowding." Proceedings of the annual convention of the Amer. Psych. Assn. 8: 211-212.

CALHOUN, J. (1962) "Population density and social pathology." Scientific Amer. 206: 139-148.

CHRISTIAN, J. J., V. FLYGER, and D. E. DAVIS (1960) "Factors in mass mortality of a herd of Sika deer (cervus nippon)." Chesapeake Sci. 1: 79-95.

DESOR, J. A. (1972) "Toward a psychological theory of crowding." J. of Personality and Social Psychology 21: 79-83.

DUBOS, R. (1970) "Physiological responses to population density," pp. 202-208 in H. M. Proshansky, W. H. Ittelson, and L. G. Rivlin (eds.) Environmental Psychology. New York: Holt, Rinehart & Winston.

ESSER, A. H. (1973) "Experiences of crowding: illustration of a paradigm for man-environment relations." Representative Research in Social Psychology 4: 207-218.

FREEDMAN, J. L., S. KLEVANSKY, and P. R. EHRLICH (1971) "The effect of crowding on human task performance." J. of Applied Social Psychology 1: 7-25.

GRIFFITT, W. and R. VEITCH (1971) "Hot and crowded: influences of population density and temperature on interpersonal affective behavior." J. of Personality and Social Psychology 17: 92-98.

GUNDERSON, E.K.E. and R. H. RAHE [eds.] (1974) Life Stress and Illness. Springfield, Ill.: Charles C Thomas.

KENDALL, G. M. and A. STUART (1966) The Advanced Theory of Statistics: Design and Analysis and Time-Series, Vol. 3. New York: Hafner.

KIRITZ, S. and R. H. MOOS (1974) "Physiological effects of social environments." Psychosomatic Medicine 26: 96-114.

LOO, C. (1973) "Important issues in researching the effects of crowding in humans." Representative Research in Social Psychology 4: 219-226.

——— (1972) "The effect of spatial density on the social behavior of children." J. of Applied Social Psychology 2: 372-381.

MacDONALD, W. S. and C. W. ODEN (1973) "Effects of extreme crowding on the performance of five married couples during twelve weeks of intensive training." Proceedings of the annual convention of the Amer. Psych. Assn. 8: 209-210.

McDONALD, B. W. and E.K.E. GUNDERSON (1974) "Determinants of job satisfaction in naval environments." J. of Applied Psychology 59: 371-373.

McGREW, W. C. (1972) An Ethological Study of Children's Behavior. New York: Academic Press.

MILGRAM, S. (1970) "The experience of living in cities." Science 167: 1461-1468.

PROSHANSKY, H. M., W. H. ITTELSON, and L. G. RIVLIN (1970) "Freedom of choice and behavior in a physical setting," pp. 173-183, in H. M. Proshansky, W. H. Ittelson, and L. G. Rivlin (eds.) Environmental Psychology: Man and His Physical Setting. New York: Holt, Rinehart & Winston.

PUGH, W. M. and L. M. DEAN (1974) "Situational and perceptual components of crowding." Presented at the annual convention of the American Psychological Association, New Orleans.

SMITH, D. C., L. M. KENDALL, and C. L. HULIN (1969) The Measurement of Satisfaction in Work and Retirement. Chicago: Rand McNally.

STOKOLS, D. (1974) "Theoretical and empirical issues with regards to privacy, territoriality, personal space, and crowding." Presented at the annual convention of the American Psychological Association, New Orleans.

——— (1972) "On the distinction between density and crowding: some implications for future research." Psych. Rev. 79: 275-277.

———, M. RALL, B. PINNER, and J. SCHOPLER (1973) "Physical, social, and personal determinants of the perception of crowding." Environment and Behavior 5: 87-115.

THIESSEN, D. D. and D. A. RODGERS (1961) "Population density and endocrine function." Psych. Bull. 58: 441-451.
ZLUTNICK, S. and I. ALTMAN (1972) "Crowding and human behavior," pp. 44-58 in J. F. Wohlwill and D. H. Carson (eds.) Environment and the Social Sciences. Washington, D.C.: American Psychological Association.

PSYCHOPHYSIOLOGICAL RESPONSES TO CROWDING

DAVID A. D'ATRI *is an NIH Postdoctoral Fellow of the Department of Epidemiology and Public Health, Yale Medical School, and Visiting Lecturer in Environmental Design, Yale School of Architecture. His research interests concern the role of psychosocial factors in chronic disease, with particular emphasis on the role of the built environment and cardiovascular disease.*

Two theories dealing with the individual's response to environmental variations are of great importance in their implication for population theory: those of Cannon (1915, 1929) and Selye (1946, 1956, 1963). Cannon placed emphasis on the secretions of the adrenal medulla, while Selye has mainly implicated the actions of the adrenal cortex.

A number of mammalian investigations suggest that the adrenal medulla plays an important role in the adaptation of groups as well as individuals. Medullary hyperplasia and hypertrophy in mice have been shown to accompany crowding (Bullough, 1952), and medullary hypertrophy has been observed in a number of species of captive wild ungulates subjected to crowding (Christian, 1960). Moreover, elevated blood sugar levels noted in rats living under conditions of crowding (Ader et al., 1963; Barnett et al., 1960) can be interpreted as evidence for catecholamine stimulation of glycogen breakdown (Turner, 1961).

A more common occurrence found in natural and confined populations which may implicate medullary secretion is a sudden increase in mortality. Crowding of animals is often followed by prostration, convulsions, and sudden death (Christian, 1960). The greater the number placed together, the greater the number which die in this fashion, even though there is a good deal of variation among populations. The proximate cause of death is not known, although the symptomatology, in some cases, is strongly suggestive of an exhaustion of adrenal medullary hormones and thus hypoglycemic shock. Green et al. (1939), working with the horseshoe hare (Lepus americanus), have reported that sudden death within large populations is accompanied by a decrease in liver starch and low blood sugar levels. Christian (1956) implicated adrenal-glandular mechanisms in the regulation of population growth. He found that the adrenal glands enlarge and that the thymus and secondary reproductive organs diminished in weight when mice are placed in groups. These changes in weight were related to the size of the population or group, and were presumably a reaction to sociopsychological pressures.

High blood pressure, the most common chronic disease worldwide in man, has been studied in association with crowding both in man and several other mammalian species.

One of the most important observations relating crowding to elevation of blood pressure was that of Henry et al. (1967). The authors found that it was possible to induce prolonged hypertension in mice by the use of psychosocial stimuli. Their methods involved: (1) mixing of animals previously housed in different boxes, (2) aggregating animals in small boxes, (3) subjecting groups to a predator, and (4) inducing conflict for territory by placing equal numbers of males and females in an interconnected box system. In the experimental situations involving the most marked type of psychosocial stimulation, the mean arterial blood pressure rose from 126 mm/Hg to the range of 150-160 mm/Hg and was sustained at this higher level for six to nine months. Those animals aggregated from birth showed less blood pressure elevation. This demonstrated that social groupings and, in effect, crowding of nonprimates could be used in the experimental approach to the role of psychosocial stimuli, and that the early environment in the etiology of human hypertension is particularly important.

Henry et al. (1971) demonstrated that psychosocial stimulation of mice affected the enzymes involved in the synthesis and metabolism of two hormones affecting blood pressure, noradrenaline and adrenaline. They found that adrenal gland weights, adrenal noradrenaline and adrenaline, monoamine oxidase, tyrosine hydroxyalase (the rate limiting enzyme in catecholamine synthesis), and phenylethanolamine-N-transferase (PNMT, the enzyme which converts noradrenaline to adrenaline) were all increased as was blood pressure in the stimulated group. A significant decrease in the two latter enzymes was observed in isolated animals.

It is suggested that the increase in the catecholamine-forming enzymes resulting from psychosocial stimulation may be mediated by the nervous system and that this response is not immediate as in the case of a sudden discharge of noradrenaline and adrenaline in stages of anger or aggression. Because these enzyme responses take several hours to develop, the data provide evidence of long-sustained adrenal medullary responses to acute episodes of social stimulation. The prolonged adrenal medullary response may result in sustained elevation of blood pressure, and subsequently, damage to organs such as the brain, heart, and kidney.

The elevation of blood pressure found in German prisoners of war after World War II suggests that crowding may be associated with increased blood pressure (Lang, 1950). Even though not collected specifically to test the effect of crowding on blood pressure, the only other data on man which support the notion that crowding is associated with increased blood pressure is that furnished by Harburg et al. (1970, 1973). They studied the effect of stress on blood pressure in overcrowded ghetto and suburban conditions in Detroit and found that the proportions of persons with hypertensive-level blood pressures were significantly greater in the overcrowded stressful tracts than in the suburban tracts. The analysis of the data implicates the psychological construct of suppressed hostility as the mechanism of coping response which is characteristic of those persons with the highest blood pressure levels.

Our work (D'Atri and Ostfeld, 1973) in this area began as an attempt to replicate in man the findings of a positive association between crowding (rather simplistically conceived at that point) and blood pressure in mammals. We wanted to test one major hypothesis: under conditions of enforced crowding there will be a positive correlation between degree of crowding and blood pressure levels.

PROCEDURE

SELECTION OF SAMPLE

The characteristics of an environment that we hypothesized to produce elevated blood pressures were: (1) a crowded environment; (2) an enforced stay in that environment; and (3) a continuous subjection to that environment. Initially, we determined that military barracks, submarines, and urban apartments did not fill all these criteria. The prison approximated most closely the human setting in which these characteristics can be found. Therefore, it was believed essential to carry out this study in prisons.

Data were collected from three correctional institutions. Each of these institutions had several modes of housing for their inmates. These institutions were also selected on the basis of the comparability of the average length of sentence of their inmates. The average age of inmates was 26. The mean length of sentence was 7 months and 71% of the inmates were white, 27% black, and 2% other.

Institution A had three modes of housing. An inmate could be in a single cell, could share a cell with one other, or could share a somewhat larger cell with three or more others.

Institution B had two modes of housing. An inmate could be in a single cell or be in one of two large dormitories.

Institution C also had two modes of housing in which an inmate could either be in a single cell or in a large dormitory.

Once the populations had been identified, collection of data was attempted from the entire enumerated population of each institution. Only those inmates in the institutions on the day in which data collection commenced were considered to constitute the study population. Cooperation rates and completion rates exceeded 90% in all institutions. Those who did not participate differed in no essential characteristic from those who did participate.

Data were collected by trained interview persons using standardized questionnaires in each institution. The forms differed slightly from institution to institution in that inappropriate items were deleted and some additional data were collected in the latter stages of the study.

The items that were collected in all three institutions included demographic and subcultural data, personal characteristics, height, weight, education, previous occupation, confinement history, mode of housing, and blood pressure determinations. In institutions B and C, data were also collected on the amount of time the inmate was out of his cell or dorm, whether or not he had a job detail (the items were inappropriate for institution A), smoking history, attitude of guards, subjective attitude of the size and crowdedness of the institution, and pulse rate. Blood pressure and pulse rate determinations in all institutions were made by another investigator "blind" to all other data collected on each participant. Before the study began, reliability studies were done on all those persons who were to perform blood pressure determinations. There was 80% agreement between blood pressure determinations (within 10 mm/Hg systolic, and 5 mm/Hg diastolic) when taken in random order on a series of 24 individuals. Blood pressure determinations were done on the left arm at the level of the right atrium after the participant had been seated for a minimum of five minutes. Phase I and phase V Korotkoff sounds were recorded to the nearest 5 or 0. The reason for this is that reliability is better with phase V than phase IV (Pickering, 1955). When hypertensive-range blood pressures were found, the participant as well as the institution was notified with the inmate's permission.

In institution C, data were also collected on furlough history, and specific complaints of inmates about the institution.

Following is a series of charts which persents some of the main findings of our cross-sectional study.

In institution A mean blood pressure, both systolic and diastolic in both black and white inmates, is higher for those housed in the dormitory as compared to those housed in either a single or double occupancy cell, although the number housed in dormitories is very small. Table 1 indicates that systolic and diastolic pressures are significantly higher for those housed in a dormitory versus those housed in a single occupancy cell, and the only significant differences in all variables compared for the total population are systolic and diastolic pressures. As can be seen, such factors as age, height, and weight, which, if substantially different, might have accounted for blood pressure differences, had no such effect here. It should be pointed out that pressures for black inmates as a group were lower than for white inmates. This finding, although surprising, may be accounted for by the facts that black inmates were younger, taller, lighter in weight, and much more likely to be recidivists than white inmates.

Similarly, the mean systolic and diastolic blood pressure in both black and white inmates is higher for those housed in dormitories than in those housed in single occupancy cells in institution B. Table 2 displays the single occupancy cell and dormitory (both institution B dormitories combined) groups and indicates that systolic and diastolic blood pressures are significantly higher for those inmates housed in dormitories as compared to those housed in single occupancy cells for all inmates. The only other variable significantly different in these groups for the total population is duration of confinement, showing that those housed in a dormitory had been confined for a longer period of time than those housed in a single occupancy cell. The relevance of duration of confinement to blood pressure will be shown later in this section.

In institution C the mean systolic and diastolic pressures are higher in white inmates housed in dormitories than in white

TABLE 1
Total Population (White and Black Inmates Combined)
Single Occupancy Cell vs. Dormitory in Institution A

Variable	Number of Cases	Mean	Standard Deviation	T Value	2-Tail Probability
Systolic BP					
GROUP I	27	109.63	17.70	3.37	.005
GROUP II	7	133.57	11.80		
Diastolic BP					
GROUP I	27	67.78	9.84	2.86	.01
GROUP II	7	79.29	7.87		
Height					
GROUP I	27	69.00	3.63	0.48	NS
GROUP II	7	68.29	2.75		
Weight					
GROUP I	27	168.04	24.27	1.11	NS
GROUP II	7	157.29	14.76		
Age					
GROUP I	27	29.44	11.91	0.27	NS
GROUP II	7	28.00	15.98		
Inst. Conf.[a]					
GROUP I	27	84.37	124.01	0.22	NS
GROUP II	7	95.71	110.95		
Total Conf.[b]					
GROUP I	27	1725.07	2645.51	0.28	NS
GROUP II	7	1432.14	1043.40		

NOTE: Group I = single occupancy cell; Group II = dormitory.
a. Duration of confinement in institution.
b. Total lifetime institutional confinement.

inmates in single occupancy cells. This relationship is also true for systolic pressures in black inmates housed in dormitories as compared to those housed in single occupancy cells, but it is not true for diastolic pressure. The number of black inmates in each of these housing modes is small, however.

The mean pulse rate for both black and white inmates is higher in those housed in the dormitory than in those housed in

TABLE 2
Total Population (White and Black Inmates Combined)
Single Occupancy Cell vs. Dormitory A and Dormitory B
Combined in Institution B

Variable	Number of Cases	Mean	Standard Deviation	T Value	2-Tail Probability
Systolic BP					
GROUP I	52	112.11	12.38		
				4.98	.001
GROUP II	39	127.31	16.73		
Diastolic BP					
GROUP I	52	68.65	7.42		
				4.94	.001
GROUP II	39	76.79	8.23		
Pulse					
GROUP I	52	76.04	9.29		
				1.43	NS
GROUP II	39	79.08	10.94		
Height					
GROUP I	52	69.61	2.83		
				0.46	NS
GROUP II	39	69.33	3.05		
Weight					
GROUP I	52	163.29	22.81		
				0.22	NS
GROUP II	39	164.44	26.87		
Age					
GROUP I	52	26.04	6.78		
				0.99	NS
GROUP II	39	27.92	11.38		
Inst. Conf. [a]					
GROUP I	52	113.73	113.75		
				2.01	.05
GROUP II	39	166.18	134.20		
Total Conf. [b]					
GROUP I	52	1137.08	1730.66		
				0.17	NS
GROUP II	39	1073.97	1847.52		

NOTE: Group I = single occupancy cell; Group II = dormitory A and dormitory B combined.
a. Duration of confinement in institution.
b. Total lifetime institutional confinement.

single occupancy cells. Table 3 exhibits data in institution C on the single cell occupancy and dormitory groups and indicates that there are significantly higher systolic and diastolic blood pressures and pulse rates in the dormitory group than in the single occupancy cell group for the general population. These

TABLE 3
Total Population (White and Black Inmates Combined)
Single Cell Occupancy vs. Dormitory in Institution C

Variable	Number of Cases	Mean	Standard Deviation	T Value	2-Tail Probability
Systolic BP					
GROUP I	97	114.90	11.88	5.83	.001
GROUP II	29	131.03	16.55		
Diastolic BP					
GROUP I	97	69.54	11.37	2.78	.01
GROUP II	29	76.55	13.63		
Pulse					
GROUP I	97	71.09	9.78	3.58	.001
GROUP II	29	78.28	8.34		
Height					
GROUP I	97	69.23	3.11	0.27	NS
GROUP II	29	69.41	3.69		
Weight					
GROUP I	97	160.57	21.34	3.08	.01
GROUP II	29	176.93	35.06		
Age					
GROUP I	97	23.14	7.21	2.17	.05
GROUP II	29	27.03	11.77		
Inst. Conf.[a]					
GROUP I	97	124.20	146.31	1.74	NS
GROUP II	29	180.79	177.34		
Total Conf.[b]					
GROUP I	97	593.92	778.84	1.62	NS
GROUP II	29	901.72	1223.85		

NOTE: Group I = single cell occupancy; Group II = dormitory.
a. Duration of confinement in institution.
b. Total lifetime institutional confinement.

differences were not significant for the black subgroup alone, but again, the number of black inmates in each housing mode is very small. Other variables that are significantly different for the total population are age and weight, indicating that those housed in the dormitory were older and heavier.

An interesting association occurred between duration of confinement and both systolic and diastolic blood pressure. This time trend suggests the operation of two factors on blood pressure during confinement: one, a factor of anxiety or novelty elevating pressure during the first two weeks in jail, and then another factor, probably related to crowding, beginning after a month's confinement and having a progressive effect thereafter in elevating pressures.

A stepwise multiple regression technique was used to determine the importance of housing mode, height, weight, age, duration of confinement, and skin color, in their association to systolic and diastolic blood pressure, within each of the three institutions. In all multiple regressions, systolic and diastolic blood pressures, age, height, weight, and institutional confinement are continuous variables. Skin color, as well as mode of housing (dormitory is always +1, while the other comparison groups, such as single occupancy cells, would be −1), is always dichotomous.

The results of the stepwise multiple regressions for systolic and diastolic blood pressure in the single occupancy cells versus dormitory groups in institution A show quite clearly that the only variable that is significant in its association to systolic and diastolic blood pressure is housing mode. The association of housing to systolic pressure is significant at the .001 level, with a simple correlation of .511; while the association of housing to diastolic pressure is significant at the .001 level, with a simple correlation of .450.

The results of stepwise multiple regressions for systolic and diastolic blood pressure in single occupancy cells versus dormitories (dormitories A and B combined) in institution B show that housing is highly significant at the .001 level in its association to systolic blood pressure, with a simple correlation of .466; and is significant at the .001 level in its association to diastolic blood pressure with a simple correlation of .464. Weight is also found to be significant at the .005 level in its association to systolic pressure, and significant at the .01 level in its association to diastolic pressure.

The results of stepwise multiple regression for systolic and diastolic blood pressures in the single occupancy cells versus dormitory groups in institution C show that housing is significant at the .001 level in its association to systolic blood pressure, with a simple correlation of .463, but is only suggestive and not significant in its association to diastolic blood pressure (p = .12). Age and weight, although not significant in their associations to systolic blood pressure, are significant at the .05 and .01 levels respectively, in their associations to diastolic blood pressure.

Tables 4 and 5 show that there is an association between the inmates' reports of degree of crowding and their attitude toward guards and blood pressure levels. Although these associations are somewhat suggestive, they are not statistically significant. Those inmates (in particular the white ones) viewing the environment as crowded and the guards as harsh tended to have higher pressures. An interesting exception, shown in Table 5, is that those who view the guards as "very easygoing" have higher pressures than all groups except the one viewing the guards as "very harsh." Psychiatric theory may explain this seeming discrepancy, i.e., those who report the guards as very easygoing may be those very repressors of aggressive feelings who are believed to have higher blood pressure.

Thus the major hypothesis that there would be an association between degree of crowding and blood pressure, systolic and diastolic, was strongly supported. Crowding, however, in our model is not a simple expression of number of square feet of floor space per inmate, since some of the men in single cells had no more square feet of floor space allocated to them than the men in dormitories. Rather, crowding is a multidimensionality incorporating physical, social, and personal variables. Men in dormitories have a much greater likelihood of threatening

TABLE 4
Mean Blood Pressure by Perception of Available Space
in Institutions B and C Combined

Very Crowded

Systolic (7)		Diastolic (7)	
121.43		74.29	
S.D. 9.45		S.D. 5.35	

White (4)	Black (3)	White (4)	Black (3)
121.25	121.67	73.75	75.00
S.D. 10.31	S.D. 10.41	S.D. 6.29	S.D. 5.00

Crowded

Systolic (69)		Diastolic (69)	
119.20		71.52	
S.D. 14.74		S.D. 9.67	

White (53)	Black (16)	White (53)	Black (16)
119.81	117.19	71.41	71.87
S.D. 15.84	S.D. 10.48	S.D. 10.07	S.D. 6.80

Quite a Bit of Room

Systolic (111)		Diastolic (111)	
118.20		71.31	
S.D. 16.41		S.D. 12.35	

White (87)	Black (24)	White (87)	Black (24)
118.68	116.46	71.61	70.21
S.D. 16.13	S.D. 17.66	S.D. 13.08	S.D. 9.38

A Lot of Room

Systolic (30)		Diastolic (30)	
118.17		72.00	
S.D. 13.86		S.D. 9.52	

White (15)	Black (15)	White (15)	Black (15)
115.67	120.67	69.67	74.33
S.D. 5.63	S.D. 18.79	S.D. 9.35	S.D. 9.42

interpersonal relations, including assault by prisoners, threats by guards, homosexual rape, and conflicts over territoriality. These kinds of conflicts are much less likely among men housed one in a cell. We believe that these aspects of crowding are related to the pressor effects. The curvilinear relationship between duration of confinement and blood pressure, and a possible

TABLE 5
**Mean Blood Pressure by Perception of Guards' Attitude
in Institutions B and C Combined**

Very Harsh

Systolic (11)		Diastolic (11)	
125.45		77.73	
S.D. 17.39		S.D. 9.05	
White (6)	Black (5)	White (6)	Black (5)
129.17	121.00	78.33	77.00
S.D. 19.85	S.D. 14.75	S.D. 8.16	S.D. 10.95

Harsh

Systolic (16)		Diastolic (16)	
122.81		71.25	
S.D. 16.93		S.D. 8.27	
White (6)	Black (10)	White (6)	Black (10)
120.83	124.00	68.33	73.00
S.D. 18.28	S.D. 16.96	S.D. 10.33	S.D. 6.75

Somewhat Harsh

Systolic (37)		Diastolic (37)	
118.92		71.08	
S.D. 19.58		S.D. 12.14	
White (23)	Black (14)	White (23)	Black (14)
121.30	115.00	71.30	70.71
S.D. 20.01	S.D. 18.91	S.D. 13.16	S.D. 10.72

Fairly Easygoing

Systolic (107)		Diastolic (107)	
117.43		70.65	
S.D. 13.90		S.D. 10.03	
White (81)	Black (26)	White (81)	Black (26)
117.78	116.35	70.62	70.77
S.D. 14.01	S.D. 13.75	S.D. 10.73	S.D. 7.57

Easygoing

Systolic (38)		Diastolic (38)	
116.45		70.53	
S.D. 12.46		S.D. 11.26	
White (36)	Black (2)	White (36)	Black (2)
116.53	115.00	70.41	72.50
S.D. 12.30	S.D. 21.21	S.D. 11.55	S.D. 3.54

Very Easygoing

Systolic (8)		Diastolic (8)	
125.62		83.12	
S.D. 15.91		S.D. 14.62	
White (7)	Black (1)	White (7)	Black (1)
124.29	135.00	82.86	85.00
S.D. 16.69	S.D. ------	S.D. 15.77	S.D. ------

explanation for it, have been described. Finally, inmates' perceptions of degree of crowding and of the attitude of guards were shown to be relevant to blood pressure levels.

There are at least two major limitations to this study. (1) The data are cross-sectional and not longitudinal; only correlations rather than causality about any relationships can be imputed. (2) Inmates were not completely assigned in a random fashion to housing mode. While available space at the time of confinement usually determined whether a prisoner was sent to a dormitory or to a single cell, other factors were probably operating. The dormitory is considered preferred housing and administrative attitudes and guards' feelings may also have affected assignment of housing modes. If, in fact, men were assigned to the dormitory as "preferential treatment," then ironically, what may have been preferential housing on the surface may have been not so preferential in respect to its physiological affects.

For these reasons, and the extremely important implications of these findings in crowded cities, offices, hospitals, and high-rise apartments, we want to try to replicate these findings longitudinally in a situation in which assignment to housing can be controlled.

In summary, the effect of stress and crowding on behavioral and physiological responses has been shown in the animal literature. Granting that the literature concerned with the behavioral effects of crowding on man is inadequate and full of subjective speculation, and the physiological literature equally deficient, I feel that it nevertheless supports the general concept that man reacts in a similar fashion.

However, the relationship of crowding to physiological or behavioral responses is by no means a simple one. It is one of the more complex relationships studied and involves numerous levels of arousal and "significant stimuli" on the one hand, and a host of physiological response mechanisms on the other.

The health implications of such a relationship for those living in urban high-rise apartments and those living in low income and elderly housing appear quite clear and challenging, but the design implications pose even a greater challenge. Given data to support health effects of certain built environments, an architect will have to weigh not only fiscal costs, but physiological ones too, in influencing his design process.

REFERENCES

ADER, R., J. KREUTNER, and H. L. JACOBS (1963) "Social environment, emotionality and aloxan diabetes in the rat." Psychosomatic Medicine 25: 60-68.

ALEXANDER, E. (1939) "Emotional factors in essential hypertension." Psychosomatic Medicine 1: 173.

BARNETT, S. A., J. C. EATON, and H. M. McCALLUM (1960) "Physiological effects of 'social stress' in wild rats. II. Liver glycogen and blood glucose." J. of Psychosomatic Research 4: 251-260.

BECKGAARD, P., H. KOPP, and J. NIELSON (1956) "One thousand hypertensive patients followed from 16-22 years." Acta Medica Scandinavica (Suppl. 312) 154, 175.

BULLOUGH, W. S. (1952) "Stress and epidermal mitotic activity. I. The effects of the adrenal hormones." J. of Endocrinology 8: 265-274.

CANNON, W. B. (1929) Bodily Changes in Pain, Hunger, Fear and Rage. (Second Edition.) Boston: C. E. Branford.

——— (1915) Bodily Changes in Pain, Hunger, Fear and Rage. New York: Appleton-Century-Crofts.

CHRISTIAN, J. J. (1960) "Endocrine adaptive mechanisms and the physiologic regulations of population growth." Lecture and review series No. 60-62, Naval Medical Research Institute, Bethesda, Maryland, 51-150.

——— (1956) "Adrenal and reproductive responses to population size in mice from freely growing populations." Ecology 37: 258-273.

D'ATRI, D. A. and A. M. OSTFELD (1973) "Stress, crowding and blood pressure in man." Proceedings of the A.P.H.A. (November 4-8): 116.

EISDORFER, C. (forthcoming) "Precursors of chronic brain syndrome in an elderly cohort." J. of Gerontology.

GREEN, R. G., C. L. LARSEN, and J. F. BELL (1939) "Shock disease as the cause of periodic decimation of the snowshoe hare." Amer. J. of Hygiene 30B: 83-102.

HARBURG, E., W. J. SCHULL, J. C. ERFURT, and M. A. SCHORK (1970) "A family set method for estimating heredity and stress. I. A pilot survey of blood pressure among Negroes in high and low stress areas, Detroit, 1966-67." J. of Chronic Diseases 23: 69-81.

HARBURG, E., J. C. ERFURT, L. HAUENSTEIN, D. CHAPE, W. SCHULL, and M. SCHORK (1973) "Socio-ecological stress, suppressed hostility, skin color, and black-white blood pressure, Detroit." Psychosomatic Medicine 35, 4 (July/August): 276-296.

HENRY, J. P., J. P. MEEHAN, and P. M. STEPHENS (1967) "The use of psychosocial stimuli to induce prolonged systolic hypertension in mice." Psychosomatic Medicine 29: 408-432.

HENRY, J. P., P. M. STEPHENS, J. AXELROD, and R. A. MUELLER (1971) "Effect of psychosocial stimulation on the enzymes involved in the biosynthesis and metabolism of noradrenaline and adrenaline." Psychosomatic Medicine 33: 227-237.

KAGAN, A. et al. (1958) "Blood pressure and its relation to coronary heart disease in the Framingham Study," in F. Shelton (ed.) Hypertension, Vol. VII, Drug Action, Epidemiology and Hemodynamics. Proc. Council for High Blood Pressure Research. New York: American Heart Association.

LANG, G. (1950) Hypertension Disease. Moscow: Medgiz.

OSTFELD, A. and R. SHEKELLE (1967) "Psychological variables and blood pressure," in J. Stamler et al., The Epidemiology of Hypertension. New York: Grune & Stratton.

PICKERING, G. (1961) The Nature of Essential Hypertension. New York: Grune & Stratton.

——— (1955) High Blood Pressure. New York: Grune & Stratton.

SAUL, L. (1939) "Hostility in cases of essential hypertension." Psychosomatic Medicine 1: 153.

SELYE, H. (1963) "Stress and adaptation." Indian Medical J. 57: 132-135.

——— (1956) The Stress of Life. New York: McGraw-Hill.

——— (1946) "The general adaptation syndrome and the diseases of adaptation." J. of Clinical Endocrinology 6: 117-230.

STAMLER, J., R. STAMLER, and T. PULLMAN (1967) The Epidemiology of Hypertension. New York: Grune & Stratton.

TURNER, C. D. (1961) General Endocrinology. Philadelphia: W. B. Saunders.

YEAKEL, E. H., H. A. SHENKIN, A. B. ROTHBALLER, and S. M. McCANN (1948) "Blood pressure of rats subjected to auditory stimulation." Amer. J. of Physiology 155: 118-127.